From the Founder of *Pillars* Ka Pou Whakahou

the invisible sentence

Verna McFelin
MNZM

A fascinating memoir from the wife of a prisoner and how her family survived outside the prison wire

wildsidepublishing.com

real stories. real hope.

Copyright ©2021 Verna McFelin

Contact:
www.vernamcfelin.com
Facebook: @VernaMcFelinAuthor

Published by Verna McFelin with Wild Side Publishing, February 2021
Email: verna.mcfelin@gmail.com
www.wildsidepublishing.com

All rights reserved. This book or any portion thereof may not be reproduced or used in any manner whatsoever without the express written permission of the director/author, except for the use of brief quotations in a book review.

Scripture taken from the Good News Translation (GNT) Copyright © 1992 by American Bible Society. Used by permission. All rights reserved.
The permission is automatic and does not have to be applied for.

Cover design, typesetting and layout: Wild Side Publishing

National Library of New Zealand (Te Puna Matauranga o Aotearoa)
Title: The Invisible Sentence

ISBN: 978-0-473-56277-9 (paperback)
      978-0-473-56278-6 (epub)

Subjects: Memoir, New Zealand Non-Fiction, Justice, Social Issues, Christian Living, Christian Teaching, Christian Ministry Resources

First printing February 2021 New Zealand
International listing March 2021 www.ingramspark.com

endorsements

I have always thought of Verna as a very 'matter-of-fact' person—practical, determined and committed to supporting the families of prisoners. In *The Invisible Sentence* Verna's personal story is made all the more powerful by her restraint. It is a story of institutional maltreatment, of bureaucratic indifference, of the traumatisation and bullying of her children, of individual acts of cruelty and generosity, of hardship, of the value of collective strength and support, and resilience and faithfulness in the face of adversity. Above all, it tells us that in this secular age, God is still in the house.

Sir Kim Workman KNZM, QSO

The book you hold in your hand will move you, surprise you and restore a faith and hope in you to never give up. Verna's story is unique and has been widely acclaimed; now it can be read in all it's raw honesty and inspiring detail.

David Collins, author of *The Storyteller*

endorsement

Even in a western democratic society, like New Zealand, Verna and her family faced terrible injustice and marginalisation. This book is the authentic story of a family that journeyed down this road. They didn't do it alone, God walked alongside them every step of the way. The McFelin family learned that, in whatever circumstances they faced, God had a redemptive plan to bring 'peace to troubled waters.'

Pastors David and Denise Cooper
Empower Church—Christchurch, New Zealand

dedication

I dedicate this book to God, my heavenly Father, my loving husband, Paul, my amazing children, Jacqui, Lisa, Ben, and Kate, and my sister-in-law, Debra, for, without you all, I would not have the pleasure of sharing my experience with the world.

And to all the many people who did not know me who prayed for us during our ordeal. We stand here today as a testimony of the many prayers of the saints that came our way at that time.

Thank you.

Verna

acknowledgements

I have to start by thanking my awesome husband, Paul, for allowing me to air his dirty laundry in the public arena. He also read all my drafts, recalled situations that I had forgotten, and gave me great advice that brought this book to fruition.

To my children Jacqui, Lisa, Ben and Kate and my sister-in-law Debra for the amazing journey we encountered together.

To Miriama Kamo for finding time in her incredibly busy schedule to contribute the Foreword for this book.

To Dave Palmer and Janette Busch and the New Zealand Christian Writers Group, Christchurch, who encouraged me and gave me great feedback and support.

To Pastor David Collins, Church Planter, Missionary, Teacher and Blogger; and Pastors David and Denise Cooper of Empower Church, who gave me spiritual advice. Thank you, Pastor Denise, for your prophetic word, "I must get this book written and out."

And to the Holy Spirit who guided and supported me from beginning to end, every step of the way.

Thank you.

contents

The Map: New Zealand—Aotearoa vi

Foreword xi

Prologue xiii

Chapter 1. The Beginning of the End 1

Chapter 2. The Damascus Road Experience 9

Chapter 3. The Big Move 13

Chapter 4. What about the Children? 17

Chapter 5. The Lolly Man 23

Chapter 6. But I Died for You 31

Chapter 7. I Will Go 35

Chapter 8. Dedicated and Baptised 39

Chapter 9. It is also Blessed to Receive 43

Chapter 10. The Food Angels 47

Chapter 11. God my Heavenly Husband and Father 53

Chapter 12. Giving up Smoking 59

Chapter 13. God Moves the Heavens 63

Chapter 14. One Day Left—then Homeless 67

Chapter 15. Ruling and Reigning 71

Chapter 16. The Adventures of Intercession 79

Chapter 17. Ask for a Million Dollars 87

Chapter 18. The Beginnings of Pillars 89

Chapter 19. Paul is Released from Prison....................... 95

Chapter 20. The Earthquake Angels 101

Chapter 21. Tea with the Governor General 107

Chapter 22. The End of the Beginning 111

My Lessons and Learnings 115

Glossary 119

Children of Incarcerated Parents 123

About Pillars 125

About the Author 127

the invisible sentence

foreword

Verna McFelin and her children moved in across the road when I was 11 years old. Her second eldest, Lisa, was my age. She was to go to my small Catholic primary school and to become my friend. What I couldn't know then was that it was Verna who was to become a force in mine and my family's lives for decades to come. Already exposed to prisons through my parents' work as Prison Chaplains, I felt neither judgement nor surprise that Lisa's father was in prison. It was just another of the many details I was learning about the McFelin whānau; they were a normal family, kind, generous and lively. But I remember listening to a story Lisa had written in class about the night the police came for her father. She wrote of the force, the terror, the trauma of her father's arrest. It was the beginning of restitution for his part in a kidnapping that had horrified the nation. He served his time. But, so too, did his family.

What Verna's work as the founder of Pillars did, was to remind New Zealanders of the innocence of the child. The birthright of every child is to be innocent. Verna's mahi found, however, that the burden of associated guilt weighs heavy on the child of an inmate. These children are over nine times more likely to end up in prison themselves. But was that path built by the parents or by a society which constantly reminds them of their vulnerability? A single parent family, one less income, more strain and anxiety, the stigma of a parent's imprisonment, the trauma of growing up in uncertainty. Where was the support, the care and love that Verna's children needed, that all children of prison inmates need?

Pillars was born to tend to that need, to show these young vulnerable people that society does care, and to highlight to them other pathways. While some might see this as a kindly charity with worthy ideals, Pillars is, in fact, a robust and determined organisation with real end goals—goals that can be measured not just in the lives of the families it deals with, but across the society it operates in. Almost every child that has been supported by Pillars so far has bucked the statistics—few of them have followed their parents into prison. The value of that intervention is immense, making our communities safer and easing the burden on our deeply flawed Justice and Corrections systems. This means fewer crimes, fewer traumatised victims, fewer expensive prison beds and fewer dispossessed children.

My family have supported Pillars for decades now. My parents, firstly, as the Kaumatua for the organisation and my older brother and I as Board member and ambassadors respectively. I remain proud of my association with Pillars. But, I am proud too of my relationship to Verna McFelin. I've known her since I was a child. Her influence on me has been humbling but it is her influence on our country which has been remarkable.

Miriama Kamo
Journalist

prologue

My introduction to the spiritual world began when I was two years old. One night, I was awakened by two transparent beings who were standing before me clothed in the armour of a Roman centurion. I knew they could cause me harm, but I did not know why, or understand who they were or how or why they were there. As I came face to face with them fear gripped me. I leapt over the cot's rails and bounded straight into my parents' bed in the hope they would go away. When I told my parents about what I had seen, they said that ghosts were in my imagination, they were not real, and it was all just a bad dream.

After that encounter the supernatural world became a big part of my life and I quickly learned not to share it with anyone. I felt I was the only one seeing such things and I bore the constant torment from the beings for many years while I lived in that house. It was a very lonely time.

At five years old I'd had enough. I thought if God were real, He surely would be stronger and protect me from the beings. So, one night with bated breath, I asked God if He were real to appear in the corner of my bedroom. I watched with apprehension as a dim light appeared and became brighter and brighter and there in the midst of it was Jesus himself. I quickly looked at Him then hid myself under the blankets. I just was not ready for that. But now I knew for sure that He was there for me and I did not have to be scared about the beings anymore. While God was around, nothing could hurt me.

the invisible sentence

I gave my heart to Jesus when I was six years old when a missionary came to my Sunday School to talk about her work in the New Hebrides. Her life and adventures fascinated me. As she spoke, I had a real burning desire to serve God and to be a missionary too but felt that could never be possible as I would never be good enough, or holy enough. Missionary work was only for special people.

When I was eight, we moved to a new house. The regular visits from the beings immediately stopped but now I was confronted with a new group of beings. These were different from the Roman Centurion ones, these were hideous, some with ugly white faces with blotches, wearing black capes and they had a disgusting stench. I was constantly woken in the night by several of them, some about 1.8 metres tall, some much smaller. They would jeer at me and enjoy picking up the end of my bed, lifting it high into the air and shaking it so hard that my head would bash violently on the headboard. By the time I had properly woken up they were always gone. This went on night after night for years and I told nobody, but deep inside, I knew God was there protecting me and that I would be all right.

All my best friends went to the same school and to the same Presbyterian Church. They were my community and I felt very safe. Their parents were my parents' friends, and we were all remarkably close knit.

I had a competitive spirit and I excelled in learning the scriptures so I could always be the best. We would learn the scriptures at Sunday School and then recite them the following Sunday to win a sticker. I strived to collect all the stickers for my book. Little did I know then that God had other purposes for me learning the scriptures so well.

Holidays were something of a treat for our family and, when I was 12 years old we had planned to take a train trip to Nelson to visit my uncle and aunt. We were sitting at the table having our soup just before leaving, our bags all packed in the hallway, when I had this sudden anxious thought that we were not going anywhere and that something terrible had just happened to my grandfather. At the table, I told my dad and mum that something was terribly wrong with Grandad and that we wouldn't be going to Nelson. Just then the phone rang. I can remember my parents both looking at each other with obvious unease. My dad answered the phone and came back and said, "Verna's right. Grandad has just had a heart attack. We won't be going to Nelson." I had several of these types of premonitions during my childhood years. Mainly ones that kept me from harm.

I left school and went to work, first at an accountant and sharebroker agency, then at the local newspaper. During that time, I met Paul. He was an apprentice plumber. I was 16 and he was 15. Two years later we were married and six months later we welcomed our eldest daughter, Jacqueline, into the world. It was 1970.

By then I had changed to be a Roman Catholic as I had been told by my parents that a mixed religion could be devastating to a marriage. It did not matter to me if I was a Presbyterian or a Catholic. As far as I was concerned, God was always with me everywhere I went regardless of what church I went to or whether I went to one or not.

the invisible sentence

one

the beginning of the end

*He pulled me out of a dangerous pit, out of
the deadly quicksand. He set me safely on
a rock and made me secure.*

Psalm 40: 2

During our early years of marriage, Paul and I purchased a farmlet in North Otago. We employed a builder and spent every moment of our time and money restoring the 120-year-old Ardgowan Homestead, which was on a four-hectare block, over a seven-year period. Paul learned some real building skills and loved working on the project. The children had a great life and had their own ponies. I bred and showed Old English Sheepdogs and was involved with the local Kennel Club and the SPCA. We started and owned a pizza parlour in Oamaru, and it was a real goldmine. It was one of the first pizza parlours in New Zealand and was on the 'foodie' trail. Buses would pull in one after another and we would have to cook and feed a bus load in 20 minutes. I would be serving three people at once and have three pizzas up my arms, then into the oven they would go. It was a busy time working day and night.

During one lunch time while I was at the pizza parlour, I got a call from the local Fire Brigade. I was told that our homestead was on fire. I was stunned. I tried to speak but nothing came out. My mind was racing. There were puppies in the wash house that had to be saved. I was grateful that the fireman did not hang up the phone so I could eventually blurt it out. My father had been in the Fire Brigade for 25 years and I was brought up very fire conscious. After the conversation I was more worried about what Dad would say rather than the house being on fire. We were underinsured but we did have some savings so proceeded to rebuild the house. We had a small mortgage, so decided to increase it if needed. The fire for Paul and me was the beginning of the end.

After the fire, my first taste of God's love came from a stranger, John Ballantyne, a pastor of a local church we didn't attend. He arrived at our place on the Sunday straight after church to help us clean up, still dressed in his suit.

Life went downhill after that. I was pregnant with my fourth child and we moved into a small house on a friend's farm that had been used for storing equipment. We sold the pizza parlour so Paul could rebuild and restore our home.

My daughter Kate was born during this time. The day she turned six weeks old, my hell began. Paul and his sister were arrested for the Gloria Kong kidnapping, leaving me with four children aged from six weeks to 12 years to care for alone.

The crime, described by the defence counsel as "the most publicised crime in living memory in New Zealand" outraged the whole country

the beginning of the end

and especially the small, ultra-conservative South Island town of Oamaru. My husband and two accomplices kidnapped young Gloria Kong at gunpoint; leaving her parents and three other relatives, bound and gagged. Thirty-six hours later, she was dumped in an isolated hay barn on the evening of 30 June, 1983. After Gloria freed herself and raised the alarm, police found her dishevelled, and in shock. I could not even imagine the unspeakable horror she must have endured during that time, and how frantic her parents must have been.

On the night he was arrested it was dark and stormy. There were continual outbursts of lightning and thunder followed by torrential rain. Paul, the four children and I were all in bed when six police detectives converged on our house. They just bowled in and started opening cupboards and searching our drawers. It was terrifying for me and the children. They took Paul into the bathroom and when they brought him out, they handcuffed him in front of our children. My eldest girl, Jacqui, started screaming, "Don't take my father away," my second daughter, Lisa, hid under the bed, my son, Ben, was in our bed watching wide eyed, and the baby, Kate, was asleep.

After they took Paul away, I pulled Lisa out from under the bed. She had jammed herself right up by the bedhead and it took my full force to pull her out. To this day, she cannot remember everything that happened. It was so traumatising for her and the other children.

Paul and his sister were arrested for the Gloria Kong kidnapping, leaving me with four children aged from six weeks to 12 years to care for alone.

The police detectives had brought a woman police officer with them to look after the children so I could go to the police station to be interviewed. After the interview they told me that Paul had been arrested for kidnapping and he would not be coming home. I was in shock, so my lawyer drove me home and, on the way, he crashed my car! I was so traumatised I cannot remember what happened when I got home, what happened to the lawyer, what I said to the children or what we did. I just remember the woman police officer leaving.

I felt extremely uncomfortable living in the house as our friends were also friends of the Kong family, so I moved out and into the home of Paul's parents.

Prior to the arrest I had been interviewed by the police several times. Little did I know that I was considered a suspect as it was discovered there was a woman involved in the crime. She was later found to be my sister-in-law. The receipt of a purchase I produced at the time the kidnapping took place, saved the day for me.

I was breastfeeding and had to take the baby with me for the interviews. It was June, the middle of winter and very, very cold. One time the baby picked up on my stress, stopped breathing and went blue, so the detectives stopped the car to revive her.

I was grateful Paul had never told me of his involvement. I hadn't asked as I had no reason to think it was him. There had been one night though when he hadn't come home. My mother-in-law and I talked together about it and we both had a gut feeling something was not right. She said that she felt like a volcano was about to blow. It turned out that Paul, his sister and two accomplices had been involved.

After the arrest hit national news, it began a journey of me dealing with shame, police, lawyers, trying to sell the half-finished house, travelling to court proceedings, and trying to remain sane. The local plumbing firm repossessed items we had purchased for the house in case we couldn't pay. On top of all that I had four children who had more going on than just their own needs being met.

The children's school was doing a project on the crime at the time and following the progress through the news media. Once everyone knew who the offenders were, they stopped it. My children were embarrassed and ashamed as well as the children and teachers at the school. So, it did not just affect us, it affected everyone we knew.

My son started bedwetting, my milk dried up, and I could not hold the baby for a while due to the trauma. It felt like the whole situation was happening to someone else. It was like I was watching a movie and I was in it.

The community in Oamaru were just wonderful to me and the children. They reached out in the streets, at school, came to where I was living and supported me where they could.

The days and weeks that followed could only be described as a living death. Our father, husband and provider had gone and I felt alone and lost. There was no time to grieve, just lots to do.

We had always worked to provide for our family. Now I found myself forced to line up at Social Welfare. It was hard to make ends meet.

We were not entitled to legal aid because we owned the homestead that we were still re-building after the fire, so I ended up selling it at a bargain basement price to cover costs. I paid out over $90,000 for Paul and his sister's legal costs. Paul and I didn't have a lot of say in the decision-making process as it took on a life of its own and I was the only one with money. Even though it was not my crime, it became my sentence.

Paul was sent to Addington Remand Prison, in Christchurch, which was 250 kilometres away. We didn't know anything about the justice system or even where the prison was. The first time we travelled to Christchurch we could not even find the prison. Prisons were not signposted. In fact, I asked some-

> **The days and weeks that followed could only be described as a living death. Our father, husband and provider had gone and I felt alone and lost. There was no time to grieve, just lots to do.**

one outside the prison and even they didn't know, so I missed my first visit.

Addington Prison was a terrible place. You were not allowed to touch each other. It was hard to maintain a meaningful conversation. We needed to talk about things like legal matters, care of the children and financial issues, it was impossible. There was a great long barrier down the centre of the room, Dads sat on one side with mum and kids on the other and a 'screw' would stand looking down on the inmates and visitors from the end of the room. During the nine months Paul was there, he never got to hold the baby until one day one kind 'screw' turned his back for just a moment so I could pass her over the barrier, so he could get a quick cuddle.

I quickly learned the prison jargon. The term 'screw' was prevalently used by the inmates, and families that visited and they were commonly referred to as that. Screw, is a term for prison officer or guard and is based on the fact that 'screw' was slang for 'key'. One of the most important functions of a prison guard or turnkey as he's often called, is to see that prisoners are locked up at the appropriate times—and that involves turning the 'screw'. The guards themselves see it as a derogatory term.

He would walk past me as my husband, not as a prisoner, and we could briefly touch. I just lived for that moment.

Other prison jargon was taken from British Cockney rhyming slang like 'trouble and strife,' which was your wife. I guess this is the flow over from the British jail system into colonial New Zealand.

The trial took place in Timaru, about 90 kilometres away from Oamaru. Paul was brought down from Christchurch to attend each day. My other sister-in-law, Debra and I would drive up from Oamaru to attend. The trial went on for five weeks and it was national news every day. I was not allowed to sit in on the court proceedings as I may be called to testify. The highlight during the trial for Paul and me was seeing each other outside of the prison. He would walk past me as my husband, not as a prisoner, and we could briefly touch. I just lived for that moment.

My parents struggled with the situation and when the newspaper arrived each evening, my mother would throw it straight into the fire. She didn't dare turn on the television because she didn't want to see the news.

Before the trial, I started to consider if I should move to Christchurch so I could be close to Paul. For generations my family had never moved out of the area, so it was a big decision, but my children also had a right to a relationship with their father.

John Ballantyne came and prayed with me and the children. He prayed like he really knew God and this impressed me. He prayed that God would comfort and strengthen us in the times ahead and that we would find a house for us in Christchurch.

At that time there were very few houses for rent there. The Christchurch Press newspaper only had about two columns of properties listed. It would be nigh on impossible for a prisoner's wife with four children and on a benefit to find accommodation, and accommodation that was affordable. But the prayer of the pastor had sparked a seed of faith and I knew that there was a house out there for us, somewhere.

> **While waiting with the crowd God spoke to me and said, "Do you really want this house, Verna?"**

I would visit Paul at the prison during the early afternoon and look for accommodation for the rest of the day. In the past, my communication with God had been all one way but God started speaking to me in a noticeably quiet way, deep inside. Once I turned up to this old house along with 30 other people who were all wanting to rent the place. It was old, cold and dilapidated, and the grass was growing up to the windows. It was also in a scary part of town. While waiting with the crowd God spoke to me and said, "Do you really want this house Verna?" I said, "No", and walked away; my first step in faith. I trusted God would find us the right house that was suitable for me and the children.

Debra and I started going house to house asking people if they knew of houses to rent. We would also drive around the streets looking for empty houses and would phone the City Council to check who owned them then approach the owners directly. But no one wanted a prisoner's wife with four children renting their properties. One day on my daily house-to-house round I found an empty rambling four-bedroom home. I peeked through the windows and all that I could see was an ironing board and a table in the centre of the living room. I left a note on the door asking if the place was for rent and said that I was desperate.

That evening I got a phone call. The owner was an IT man who was a workaholic and worked days and nights. He said that the house was always cold because it wasn't lived in, and the very next day he was going to go down to the Salvation Army to see if there were a family needing accommodation who could come and warm it up. He said we could have the house. The agreement was rent free accommodation in exchange for a cooked meal and ironed shirts. The house was half a block from the prison so we could walk there daily. Paul could even hear me calling the cat from his prison cell.

Debra, the children and I, lived in the house for the nine months that Paul was on remand, awaiting trial and sentence. It was a difficult time. The local prison support organisations appeared to have no understanding or support in place for families. That is the reason I started Pillars at a later date. The children had few friends and were bullied at school. They were called jail birds. Jacqui struggled and ended up on the streets twice overdosing from drugs. There was nothing I could do. At 12 years old the situation was hard on her. My family was falling apart, money was short and visits to the prison were often stressful. There were visits to lawyers who were constantly demanding increasingly large amounts of money and playing competitive games among themselves. I had to do a lot of the running around for them in preparation for the trial. Looking back, they were the biggest cause of any pressure. Life revolved around the lawyers who made all of the decisions even when it didn't seem right. Subsequently, we changed lawyers three times.

two

the damascus road experience

Peace is what I leave you;
It is My own peace that I give to you.
I do not give it as the world does. Do not be
worried and upset; do not be afraid.
John 14:27

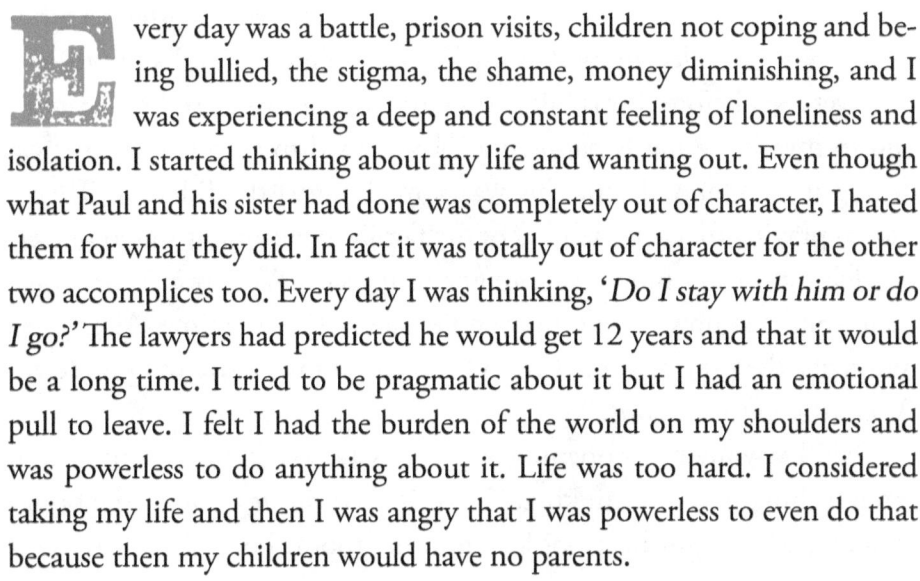very day was a battle, prison visits, children not coping and being bullied, the stigma, the shame, money diminishing, and I was experiencing a deep and constant feeling of loneliness and isolation. I started thinking about my life and wanting out. Even though what Paul and his sister had done was completely out of character, I hated them for what they did. In fact it was totally out of character for the other two accomplices too. Every day I was thinking, '*Do I stay with him or do I go?*' The lawyers had predicted he would get 12 years and that it would be a long time. I tried to be pragmatic about it but I had an emotional pull to leave. I felt I had the burden of the world on my shoulders and was powerless to do anything about it. Life was too hard. I considered taking my life and then I was angry that I was powerless to even do that because then my children would have no parents.

That was when I started going through Jacqui's Good News Gideon

Bible that she had been given at school, trying to find answers. But the Bible had so many words, and I didn't know where to look. I remembered the words of my mother, that when you marry, you marry for life. The Bible kept confirming this. But there was a great war going on in my spirit.

Then, one day about eight months after the nightmare began, I had a normal housewife's day. I got up, cleaned the house, made the lunches and vacuumed. The children went to school and came home happy. I visited Paul and he was okay. I went to bed that night and spoke to God and said, "Thank you Lord for my great day." It was the first time in my life I had ever thanked God for anything. I was not a prayerful person in the way I thought prayer was, then I lay back on my pillow and pondered about my normal day.

The next moment my room filled up with a thick bright white cloud, like nothing I had ever seen before. I was blinded by the light as it was so bright…

That's when, like Paul the Apostle, I had a Damascus Road experience. The next moment my room filled up with a thick bright white cloud, like nothing I had ever seen before. I was blinded by the light as it was so bright, and I said to myself, '*What is happening?*' I was used to spiritual experiences during my childhood, but this was something vastly different. Then I started praying for each member of my family. Beautiful, inspired prayers just fell out of my mouth. I thought to myself, '*Wow this is amazing*', then wondered how I could pray and think at the same time. After a few moments, the praying ceased and I lay back on my pillow and pondered, '*What was all that about?*'

Then I saw my heart opening as if it was a book and fire from heaven came rushing in. I am thinking, '*What is this? But it is nice.*' The bright white cloud brought heaps of love into the room. Love like I had never felt before. It just kept coming and coming in waves and I felt a real joy and peace that was inexplicable. Then within the light God Himself stepped out and walked up to my side. He leaned over toward me and spoke audibly in the gentle softest voice that I have ever heard. He said, "Peace I leave you; I leave you with peace." Being not sure about what was happening and struck with wonder about it, I said a quick, "Thank you God." I was not scared but I had a real feeling of awe as I met the Almighty God.

There was so much joy in my spirit that I got up out of bed and danced around the house. It felt as if I had lost a tonne of weight. All the burdens I had been carrying for so long had lifted. I wrote a letter to my grandmother, who I trusted the most about spiritual matters, I told her about what had happened but screwed it up the next day as I thought I was going mad. My understanding was that God only spoke to people in the Bible that way. If I let anyone know they would surely take my children away and then they would not have any parents. God just does not talk to people like that. I had learned as a child to keep quiet about such matters and decided that this also could not be shared.

After the experience I became a changed person. I was freed from the unforgiveness in my heart and the hate I had toward Paul and his sister. I got on top of my circumstances and I knew God was calling me for a purpose that I did not yet know. Where I had known about God, I now knew and loved God, and He loved me. I saw my life in a new and exciting way. I decided that churches were dead and judgmental, and I would never get involved in them.

After the experience I became a changed person. I was freed from the unforgiveness in my heart and the hate I had toward Paul and his sister.

So, it became a journey of 'woohoo', what is around the corner? What have You got for us today? And it became an excitement. I describe my relationship with God like Pooh and Tigger. We are best friends and go places together.

Paul was found guilty at the trial. Sometime later he was sent to Auckland in the North Island for sentencing. We were told he would come back to Christchurch, but he never came back. He was sentenced on the 11 April, our 13th wedding anniversary to 11 years in prison and sent to Mt Eden prison for a day then out to Paremoremo, North of Auckland. This is New Zealand's most notorious maximum-security prison. He was put into B Block predominantly with the Mongrel Mob.

My close friends, Allan and Colleen Rakiraki, were amazing. They had helped me so much after the arrest. They came up from Oamaru and arrived unexpectedly to be with me on the day of the sentencing. I was so grateful because it was a hard day. I heard what sentence Paul had got through the news. It was all over the television and the newspapers. No official person phoned and told me.

Colleen and Allan took me out for coffee in the city to get me away from it all. In the coffee shop everyone was talking about the crime and some were saying that they knew our family. Little did they know that the offender's wife was sitting in that same café listening to everything they said. On every street corner the newspaper boys selling the daily news were calling out, "Kidnappers sentenced today. Kidnappers sentenced today."

> **Little did they know that the offender's wife was sitting in that same café listening to everything they said.**

three

the big move

*Trust in the Lord with all your heart.
Never rely on what you think you know.
Remember the Lord in everything you do,
and He will show you the right way.*

Proverbs 3:5-6

I started thinking about what I was going to do now. Stay in Christchurch or move to Auckland. Do I move the children again? I didn't know a soul in Auckland let alone the North Island, except for an uncle and aunt in Wellington, but that was miles away.

I travelled to Auckland to visit Paul and after visiting I drove around to find rental accommodation. I didn't want to rent in the city as we were small town folk, so I hired a rental car on the credit card and went to find a country place north of Auckland fairly near the prison, and I came across the small town of Orewa.

I thought, *'Aw, this is a lovely place and the people here are friendly.'* The town had a nice energy. This is where we could live. It was about a half hour drive from the prison so visits could easily be managed. I walked into a real estate agent's office and asked if they had any houses to rent in the area.

the invisible sentence

"No, you'll never find anything to rent here. We've got a waiting list of 26 people looking for houses. You just can't get houses in this area at all," she said.

Just then the phone rang, and she excused herself to answer it. I just stayed put. When she had finished the call she said, "That person I was just talking to has a house to rent and I can't be bothered going through the list of 26 people, so you can have it."

So we got a house right there and then. It was in Whangaparaoa out on the peninsula and totally suitable for our needs.

I returned to Christchurch to prepare for the move. By this time, I was totally reliant on my benefit money to fly us up and to move the furniture. I had asked Social Welfare for help with removal expenses, but they would not support me as they said I should leave my husband and not move north. I asked God for help and I then kept receiving money in my letterbox from where I don't know. I had just enough with the benefit and the letterbox money to get us and our furniture to Auckland with nothing left over. At this stage we hadn't sold the homestead so money was short.

> **That person I was just talking to has a house to rent and I can't be bothered going through the list of 26 people, so you can have it.**

We arrived at the Whangaparaoa house with only a bag of potatoes, a bag of flour, a few canned foods, our sleeping bags and a few plates and cups. I didn't know anyone to ask for food and didn't even know where I could get food other than the supermarket, and you had to have money for that. We lived mainly on flour and potatoes for seven days. We had no money. I just had enough petrol in the rental car to get me to prison visits and back.

Through Paul, I found out about a social service agency that could help. I made an appointment and asked for a food parcel to get us through to the next benefit payment, but they said it was their policy to send a cheque, not give out food. The cheque would need to be countersigned by a trustee and then they would post it. So, I went home with nothing and the cheque arrived in the post about four days later. I went to cash it and it bounced. I phoned them from a phone box, as we didn't have a phone, to say that this cheque is no good, so they sent me another one. In the meantime, the benefit came in so we were able to get a few groceries. Then, the second cheque arrived and it bounced too. Luckily, I'd kept the first cheque, so I tried it at the bank again and it worked. I don't think some agencies realise how critical it is to get their systems right.

We lived happily in the house for six months then had to vacate it as our landlord was going to use it for holiday makers during the Christmas season. Landlords rented their houses out for megabucks so it was only available to us during the off season.

By then, I had met people through neighbourhood networks. They put out a call through the community for another house for us. I ended up finding one for rent near the beach and it was a brand-new unit. The deal was that I could get it quite reasonably as long as I looked after the grounds and the back unit, which was the landlord's holiday home. So, we moved in.

the invisible sentence

four

what about the children?

But Jesus called the children to Him and said, "Let the children come to me and do not stop them, because the Kingdom of God belongs to such these. Remember this! Whoever does not receive the Kingdom of God like a child will never enter it.

Luke 18:16-17

My daughter Lisa, was only nine when the police took Paul away. "I automatically thought I would never see him again. You feel a lot of hatred," she said. "It's true the children pay for the crimes of their parents." She still loved him because he was her dad, but she hated him for what he did.

The father of a close friend of hers banned all further contact with Lisa when Paul was arrested. It wasn't until secondary school that she met another girl with a father 'inside'. She says, "It's a real relief for kids to talk to someone who understands. Children need to know they are not going to be criminals just because their parent is."

Lisa recalls the first prison visit that took place at the Addington Remand Prison. She described it as horrific. "Everything looked worse than you see in the movies. You could feel the coldness, seeing her dad sitting there and not being able to touch him, going through metal detectors, hearing metal doors clanging in front of you and behind you, it really makes you jumpy and scared. The wardens really freaked me out, their faces were as cold as concrete."

She says inmates' children often have problems with their schoolwork, commit crimes in a bid to be with dad, and contemplate suicide.

She was resentful that Paul was safely in prison not having to worry about where the next meal was coming from, while the rest of the family struggled to survive. "Everyone else had flash clothes but we didn't. If my dad were home, we would have."

As the sentence progressed, it became increasing hard on the children, especially at school.

Lisa tried shoplifting, once stealing togs and towel because she couldn't be bothered going home to get her own swimming gear. "If Dad hadn't been taken away, I would never have done it. I thought he was having it really easy, so I didn't care if I got sprung and put in jail."

"It's important for parents to tell children the truth about the crimes they are charged with. I felt my dad wouldn't do that, he's too good. He wouldn't hurt anyone. It wasn't until just before he was released that I accepted it. I had to ask him. I would have liked to have known from the beginning."

As the sentence progressed, it became increasing hard on the children, especially at school.

I always told the schools that the children's father was in prison. Overall, the school teachers were incredibly supportive, and one school was excellent and went out of their way to help our children, but some of the other children and their parents weren't quite so understanding.

Ben started school when he was five. He had been really looking forward to it. He was a sociable little guy and loved making friends. The kids at school were very friendly and asked him to come out to play at the break. My son was excited that he had friends only after one day. One of the children said we are going to play cops and robbers and said, "You are going to be the robber because your dad is in jail." He was heartbroken. The bullying started right from the first day.

Jacqui would not go to school even after I saw her off on the school bus. Some months later I was contacted by the truancy officers as, unknown to me, she wasn't attending school at all. I would then have to drive 10 kilometres with my small children in the car to take her to her high school, to drop her off and watch her go into school each day. Little did I know at the time, she would just disappear again out the back door.

The school counsellor came out and brought me a pot plant and empathised with my situation. There appeared nothing anyone could do. Thankfully, they decided not to prosecute.

There was no Children and their Families Act then so if she got into crime and got arrested, I would be classed as an unfit mother and I could lose all my children.

> **One of the children said we are going to play cops and robbers and said, "You are going to be the robber because your dad is in jail."**

I had to think fast about how I could ensure that I would not lose my children. I rang Social Welfare and a social worker came out. I laid everything on the line and said I have a wayward daughter who I cannot control. Does this mean that if she gets arrested will I lose all my children? She said "Yes, you may." I said, "You tell me. What can I do?" She said, "I don't know, I can't." I said, "I want that in writing," and she gave it to me right then and there. I thought if I ever ended up in the courts, I would produce the letter as evidence of trying hard to keep my children safe. As it turned out, my daughter did not get arrested.

My daughter's behaviour was the result of the situation we found ourselves in. She had her own pony in Oamaru and was involved in the Pony Club. She was an excellent rider and won prizes at the shows. She had to leave all of that behind. During the trial, the pony had a foal and it drowned in our pond. She was talking to me the other day (she is now 50 years old) and she said, "So many people tried to help me, but I pushed them away. There was even a nice police officer who tried to help but I could not be reached. I didn't even know what I wanted myself."

Trying to keep the children in school was a full-time undertaking. On top of that, my children constantly moved schools as we moved around, and they missed out on some major opportunities. During the seven years Paul was in jail the children attended twelve different schools.

Lisa was an exceptionally good long-distance runner and had been chosen to represent the area in Auckland for running and, because of moving again she turned it down.

Even though the children's education was important to me, I was so caught up in a heightened state of survival that, unfortunately, I put education a way down the list.

During the seven years Paul was in jail the children attended twelve different schools.

Each time we moved the children had difficulty making friends. Jacqui mixed with other children who were also isolated or ostracised. Lisa had a best friend in Orewa and when we eventually moved back to Christchurch, she had another best friend across the road.

She told her friend's dad that her dad worked for the government. She figured it wasn't a lie as she thought, "Well he does in a way because he works in the prison and gets a small payment." She had learned that telling people that her dad was in prison was not a good idea if she wanted to make and keep friends.

One day her friend's dad invited her over for tea to meet his friends. He also worked for the government so was keen to know what department Lisa's dad was working for. So, at the dinner table in front of his friends, he asked Lisa, "Where does your dad work?" Lisa did not know what to say so she just blurted out, "My dad is in prison."

He then said to her "You have just embarrassed me in front of my friends. Leave the table and don't expect to play with my daughter again."

That was the last time she spoke to her friend.

Another time Lisa was in a bus with children going on a school trip and one of the children yelled out in front of everyone, pointing, "Her father's in jail." The teacher was embarrassed not knowing what to say or do. My daughter stood up and said to the whole bus, "My dad is in prison and I love him very much. He might have done something wrong, but I am looking forward to him coming home," and everyone went quiet. It was lucky I had taught the children skills about how to cope when these situations arose.

When Kate started school, Paul was already into the fifth year of his imprisonment. She walked to school as it was just in the next block. At school she met a friend, Vicki, who also had a dad in prison. They became awfully close and were called Cake and Bickie. They are still close friends today.

I am so proud of my children and how they got through in the end. The three girls went to university as adults to study and gain qualifications in nursing, psychology and teaching and my son has his own business. As well as that they bring their life experiences with them, which has been crucial in their professions. They are all highly empathetic and more in touch with people's needs and are a blessing to all they meet.

the invisible sentence

five

the lolly man

Then the King will say to the people on His right, "Come, you that are blessed by my Father! Come and possess the kingdom which has been prepared for you ever since the creation of the world. I was hungry and you fed me, thirsty, and you gave me a drink; I was a stranger and you received me in your homes, naked and you clothed me; I was sick and you took care of me, in prison and you visited me."

The righteous will answer him, "When Lord, did we ever see you hungry and feed you, or thirsty and give you a drink? When did we ever see you a stranger and welcome you in our homes, or naked and clothe you? When did we see you sick or in prison and visit you?"

The King will reply, "I tell you, whenever you did for one of the least important of these followers of mine, you did for me!"

Matthew 25:34-40

the invisible sentence

Paremoremo Prison was a formidable place. It was seven kilometres out from Albany which was inland off State Highway 1. There was no public transport. We would get the bus from Whangaparaoa to Albany and I would walk to the prison pushing a pushchair, children in tow, often in torrential rain. One day we arrived at the gates bedraggled and wet. The guards did not see us from the tower as we were not in a motor vehicle, so they didn't put up the barriers to let us in. Another motorist had to alert them to us so we could get in.

We enjoyed our visits together as a family. Paul never told me much about what went on in prison. I know he went into prison survival mode, but I did hear when major happenings took place like when an inmate committed suicide, (they were usually friends) or if there had been a lock down or some other prison drama.

We never discussed the crime except Paul said that he didn't know why he got involved. "It was just one bad night" that culminated from a series of happenings that affected him, the homestead fire, the rebuilding of the homestead, the selling of the pizza parlour, the selling of his mustang motor vehicle and the birth of a new baby. There was no reasonable excuse. Even though one of the accomplices asked for a $120,000 ransom, we had no financial problems and we were quite comfortably well off.

We never discussed the crime except Paul said that he didn't know why he got involved. "It was just one bad night..."

The inmates in B Block were hugely supportive of me. Along with the prison environment, Paul had to contend with the new me. I was full on talking about God as he was my only companion on the outside. It was all about Him. By then Paul had experienced His goodness as well and had seen some miracles take place within prison walls, so he was encouraging. However there was a question from the superintendent about all the scripture and Christian literature that was being sent in—he asked about my well-being and how Paul felt about it. Paul had already discussed it with the inmates who were the leaders within the Mob and they gave him the best of advice. "What would you rather her do Nap (that was his prison nickname, short for kidnapper), get into God or be lifting her skirt on Queen Street (Queen Street in Auckland is where the prostitutes hang out)?" A lot of partners ended up on the streets to feed their children. A number of them ended up with drug habits.

While waiting for visits at Paremoremo I met six other women who were also visiting their partners. We formed a bit of an informal support group. One woman came from Waiheke Island and would ferry into Auckland and bus out to Albany. Another woman would arrive who had obviously suffered from physical violence, and there were others. None of us went without because we would look out for each other. We all knew how important and sacred the weekly visit was and knew it could not be missed.

One day the woman from Waiheke Island arrived having money for only one fare over and expecting the group to get her back home. We just put the 'hat' around. I had been given $20 I didn't need at the time and that went into the hat and between us we came up with enough to get her back home. I thought at the time, *'Isn't this just great. Wouldn't it be wonderful if there were this type of support for partners and families in every prison?'*

This was the spark that started me thinking about the much-needed support for families and children living in the shadows of the prison world.

Trying to maintain family relationships behind bars was not easy. My estimation is that 90% of prisoners in relationships at the start of a 'long lag' are in the lonely-hearts club by the end of it. I watched other families disintegrate as the stress of maintaining relationships from prison became too much. On the one hand, the government was hell bent on providing supported accommodation for prisoners on release but on the other, would not support and uplift the family and whānau unit as a place for prisoners to return home to. The key to cutting the recidivism rate is ensuring that these people maintain stable family and whānau ties while in prison and so they can repair and retain family relationships on release.

> **The key to cutting the recidivism rate is ensuring that these people maintain stable family and whānau ties while in prison and so they can repair and retain family relationships on release.**

With figures showing that imprisonment costs, on average, $91,000 a year per inmate and, with the expectations of continuing increases in our crime rate, the focus on the skills that keep families together and lower offending has never been so important. The grim alternative is to keep building more prisons and have family and whānau relationships break down.

For the children, they were just pleased to see their dad when they visited. It didn't matter to them that he was in a prison. The main issue was that they had to sit on cold hard seats in a stark environment for hours, which was impossible for the little ones. As long as Dad was okay, they were fine.

Once we were rushing to the visit and it was in the middle of my baby's bottle feed. I walked through to the 'sally port' and I was carrying the baby still feeding from the bottle. The guard on duty said, "You can't take that bottle in there," and he started yanking the bottle out of the baby's mouth and said, "You've got to go in there without the bottle." So, we had a screaming baby right through the visit.

Another time, the baby pooed herself. So, I asked if I could just go out of the visiting room to change the baby and come back and they said, "Yes sure." So, I went out to change the baby, and when I came back they wouldn't let me back into the visit as they had terminated it, so I only had half a visit and didn't get to say goodbye to Paul.

I had two friends in Whangaparaoa who also happened to be prison visitors. One friend was a church visitor who attended church services at the prison and, the other, a volunteer for Prisoner's Aid.

My church friend could meet with my husband and have communion with him, worship with him and take him flowers. And the Prisoners Aid friend could meet with my husband and visit him in his cell and see him there. As his wife, married at that time for 14 years, I could do none of those things. It all seemed so wrong. Visits took place during afternoon tea time and we couldn't even have a cup of tea together. A big tea cart came around giving the inmates their hot drink, but there was none for the families, some of whom having travelled long distances.

When my mother-in-law died, I couldn't get hold of the prison for them to tell Paul, so I turned up to visit that day and I asked the guards at the door if I could please have a special visit. I had built up a lot of frustration about my treatment at prison visits so I would get quite abrupt at times. They said, "What do you want a special visit for?" I said very loudly, "My husband's mother has died!"

I was thinking, *'I will fix you.'* They went very sympathetic and straight away put me onto the prison chaplain, Father John Moss, who organised a special visit away from the visiting room for us, right there and then.

Paul and I needed to attend the funeral, but to get him out of a maximum-security prison would be difficult.

I spoke to God and asked him, "What should I do?" He immediately said, "Ask Paul's lawyer. (Our team of lawyers were incredibly supportive and helpful at this time)." So, before I could change my mind and find that too hard of a task, I dialled the number and asked the lawyer. He said, "Yes, just tell the prison that I will cover all the expenses." So, I contacted the prison and informed them. This would include his airfares and transport from Auckland to Oamaru, and a prison guard, with his expenses, to attend with him. The offer from the lawyer was out of this world. Then there were my expenses to get to Oamaru and find caregivers for my children in Whangaparaoa. I was blessed that this all came about.

At the last minute, it was decided by higher ups, that Paul was too big of a risk and he should not attend the funeral. The inmates right across the prison 'propped' to get Paul out for the funeral. I got a phone call from Father John Moss letting me know that the whole prison had 'propped', and that Paul was all right.

Whether it was through the 'prop' or not, a Government ministerial decision was made that Paul could attend his mother's funeral but I would have to pay for an extra guard. One had to be a D Block guard and the other, a Chief Officer.

Generally, Paremoremo was a great place for visits, it was the opposite of Paparua in Christchurch. The guards at Paremoremo sat in a glass area nicknamed 'the goldfish bowl' and you were free to have a visit without interference, but at Paparua Prison in Christchurch you had the guards standing over you during the visits making it difficult to have family conversations.

The younger ones would get bored after 15 minutes and spend the next two hours racing around. They would line up chairs with the other children and push them around like a train. There were no toys or activities to keep them occupied and no support for child and parent bonding. Parents were forever getting reprimanded for not looking after their children and ultimately, visits were terminated for some.

Prison visiting back then was not at all family friendly and the children were often scared of the guards, the heavy doors, and being locked in.

Lisa had been interviewed by a newspaper at some stage and they asked her about prison visits. It was reported that she said the guards had faces like stone. When she went out to visit the following week, one of the guards took her to task about it unbeknown to me. He harassed her about it and said, "What's the idea of talking about us like that?" She was twelve years old.

Parents were forever getting reprimanded for not looking after their children and ultimately, visits were terminated for some.

When Paul eventually got transferred to Rolleston minimum-security prison, the privacy at visits was even worse. If you got too close the guards would come up and say, "Step apart." I managed to cope because my spiritual relationship with God overrode my emotional needs. I was blessed that God did this for me.

Year in and year out when we visited Rolleston prison we would watch the magpies outside of the visiting room window. We saw generations of magpies come and go. That was our special family activity together.

There was only one swing for all the children visiting. I could not see the logic of it. The room was not family friendly at all and it was difficult trying to maintain a family relationship.

Paul would use his small allowance from working in the prison to buy sweets for the children when they visited. He used to smuggle them out chocolate. This was something the children never had at home. Kate used to call him the Lolly Man as this is only how she knew him. Because she was six weeks old when he went to prison, she had never known him as Dad at home. Now she was seven years old and she thought he was the nice man who gave her lollies.

After visits we would all go through a real low and nothing much was spoken in the car on the way back home. The children would often cry as they did not want to leave their dad behind. My nine-year-old son used to hold my hand when I was driving to and from visits. He understood it was an emotional time for all of us.

six

but I died for you

*But God has shown us how much he loves us—
it was while we were still sinners,
that Christ died for us!*

Romans 5:8

I couldn't wait to get into bed each night, when the house was quiet to spend quality time with God.

There was so much blessing and comfort coming from Him and it was full on. Most of my talking with God now, was thanking Him for what he was doing in our lives. He was meeting all our needs. I was overawed by His goodness.

I found it easy to read the Bible and it started speaking to me by the words jumping off the pages. I discovered that the Bible was not your ordinary everyday book but that it contained a power. The promises within the Bible became, *Yes and Amen… 2 Corinthians 1:20. That is, what was said was true and would happen. And if that were not true, is God a liar? God is not people, who lie. He is not a human who changes his mind. Whatever he promises, he does; He speaks, and it is done* –Numbers 23:19

the invisible sentence

I remember reading, *So also will be the word that I speak—it will not fail to do what I plan for it; it will do everything I send it to do* – Isaiah 55:11. I remembered those many years ago when I was learning the scriptures at Sunday School to get stickers for my book, God had other ideas. Even though I was reading the Good News Bible, God was speaking to me in my spirit in the old King James version I had learned as a child. Those scriptures had remained in my spirit all those years. I could recall them in an instant. Reading the Bible was like getting a love letter from God. During the early days of my walk, I 'burned out' quite a few Bibles.

In the Bible it talks about speaking in tongues. I didn't know what that was, except it was a funny language and it happened to people in the Bible on the day of Pentecost.

One night I was talking to God and thanking Him, and I got quite overtaken and I said, "I just can't thank you enough, there are just not words to express how I feel," and I started to speak in tongues, and it felt really amazing. I just seemed to be filled up with glory. So, I did this a lot because it felt so good and it seemed to recharge me and keep me on top of things. Day and night, and in front of the children, I would get about the house speaking in tongues.

> **I had made a decree to God that I was never going back to a church because they were all dead and judgmental places and the God I now knew and loved was not in them, but I now discovered otherwise.**

Lisa was talking to her friend at school about her mother speaking in this funny language to God and her friend said, "So does my mine." He went home and told his mother. As soon as he told her she came straight down to my place.

Margaret Mikkelsen was my introduction to church and church life. I had made a decree to God that I was never going back to a church because they were all dead and judgmental places and the God I now knew and loved was not in them, but I now discovered otherwise. I thought I was the only one who heard God speak and I didn't know that there were others out there too. I discovered a whole group of people at the Hibiscus Coast Inter-fellowship and they were all like me. Even my local priest, Father Peter Gray was involved. We held church on a Sunday night in a hall and everyone who loved God used to go. It did not matter what denomination you came from. They were my community that really looked after me and the children. They would often come around to see if I was okay. Even things like fixing my washing machine and making sure it was balanced.

The children also went to the Inter-fellowship and they brought their friends, and their friends brought their friends.

> **Even with all of this going on in my life I could not accept the fact that Christ died for me. I believed Christ died for everyone else but not me. I did not feel worthy of anything like that.**

Even with all of this going on in my life I could not accept the fact that Christ died for me. I believed Christ died for everyone else but not me. I did not feel worthy of anything like that. I was a single mum bringing up four children with a husband in prison. I was a nobody. Why would Christ die for me or even that I would really matter to Him?

Every Sunday morning I would go to the Catholic Church and then to the Inter-fellowship in the evening. One week, the message at the Catholic Church was about Christ dying for us; but I didn't accept that message was for me. That evening I went to the Inter-fellowship and the message was about Christ dying for us, but I didn't accept that message was for me. Later in the week I went to a Women's Aglow meeting and the message was about Christ dying for us, but I still didn't accept that the message was for me.

Driving home after the Women's Aglow meeting I was very unhappy that I had heard the same message three times in a row that didn't appear to be for me, and I told God so. I was thirsting for knowledge about everything I could know about God, so the three similar messages appeared to be a waste of learning.

Driving home in my car, I distinctly remember hearing His still, quiet voice saying, "But I died for **YOU**."

The realisation hit me. I pulled over as my eyes welled up with tears. "So, you really did die for me?"

Jesus said, "Yes, I died for you. If you were the only person in the world, I would have still died for you. I paid the price. I arranged those three messages for you until you had got it."

seven

I will go!

> *I said, "There is no hope for me! I am doomed because every word that passes my lips is sinful, and I live among a people whose every word is sinful. And yet, with my own eyes I have seen the King, the Lord Almighty." Then one of the creatures flew down to me, carrying a burning coal that he had taken from the altar with a pair of tongs. He touched my lips with the burning coal and said, "This has touched your lips, and now your guilt is gone, and your sins are forgiven." Then I heard the Lord say, "Whom shall I send? Who will be our messenger?" I answered, "I will go! Send me!"*
>
> Isaiah 6:5-8

At the time, some in the Catholic Church were experiencing charismatic revival, as were many in other denominations. As it turned out the prison chaplain, Father John Moss was also running the movement. I had some church friends who warned me off it while other friends embraced it. It seemed like a good thing to me, so I decided to get involved. The church was running some courses on making God more real in your life and I decided to go.

The first session was about giving our heart to God and giving your life to Him. I had already done that, but the course offered something new. It offered me an opportunity to find my purpose and calling. At the second session, a scripture was read about Isaiah being called to be a prophet. I wondered if I too could be called to do something special for God too.

As the scripture was being read, I heard God's small voice saying, "Stick out your tongue." I thought, *'This is embarrassing. Do I really want to do this in front of all these people? I hardly know them.'* Then I thought, *'Well, God has said so, so I'd better do as I am told.'* So, with great trepidation and embarrassment I stuck out my tongue with everyone watching and right there and then felt a sense of burning on my lips and tongue. A Seraphim himself had come and placed that exact live coal on my lips and I said out loud, "Here I am Lord. Send me."

I learned through that experience that God wanted my embarrassment and shame too. I had plenty of that to give. Being a prisoner's wife, I struggled with shame. There was another time where God challenged me when I went to a Bill Subritzky meeting and he got a word of knowledge about someone in the congregation having piles (haemorrhoids). I knew the word was for me. I had struggled with piles for years. I had a choice, keep them, or stand up in front of 500 people and reveal to them all that it was me with the piles. I stood up and was instantly healed and they have never come back to this day. That was also the day that shame left me.

My relationship with God got a lot more serious after that. His voice was so soft and still and I did not want to miss it. I needed to keep a clear mind and keep a strong focus on Him so I would not miss anything He was saying, as it could be especially important, and people could be at risk if I didn't respond.

There were three keys I found transformational. The first one was a special prayer I prayed that if I ever stepped out of God's will that He would override my will. I did not trust myself. This prayer brought a lot of grace into my life and God would often remind me of it. I grew in confidence that I was always in God's will and I could trust Him to keep me in it. Not only that, but God was also gracious and would let me know in advance when something appeared to be outside of his will when, in fact, it wasn't.

> **I knew I was being called to help other prisoners' wives and children so I bravely prayed and asked God to give me every pain, experience and burden these women were carrying...**

The second key was how to get rid of my own thoughts and keep my mind uncluttered so that they would not get in the way of God's voice. I read a scripture that said,

We pull down every proud obstacle that is raised against the knowledge of God; we take every thought captive and make it obey Christ –2 Corinthians 10:5.

When I had difficulty focussing on prayer, I would pray this scripture to bring my thoughts into captivity; and it really worked.

A third key was that to do His will I needed to be prepared to give myself totally to Him. I knew I was being called to help other prisoners' wives and children so I bravely prayed and asked God to give me every pain, experience and burden these women were carrying so I could say to them, "Yes, I know how it feels. I have experienced that myself." I asked Him to "bring it all on." That prayer bought an element of high risk, but with it came high grace.

But His answer was, *"My grace is all you need, for my power is greatest when you are weak." I am most happy, then, to be proud of my weakness, in order to feel the protection of Christ's power over me* —2 Corinthians 12:9.

I found that through Christ I could do great things, impossible things. Whatever gifts and experiences (good or bad) I had been given and was experiencing; they came with a God-purposed plan alongside.

eight

dedicated and baptised

"Go, then, to all peoples everywhere and make them my disciples: baptise them in the name of the Father, the Son, and of the Holy Spirit, and teach them to obey everything I have commanded you. And I will be with you always, to the end of the age."

Matthew 28:19-20

At the Hibiscus Coast Inter-fellowship someone had a word of knowledge that I was to bring my two youngest children, Ben, who was four, and Kate, who was two, up to the front of the congregation. I was cradling them on my knees while sitting on the floor and next thing they were touched by the power of God. They looked so beautiful with their eyes closed and glowing in God's love. God showed me that I was dedicating them to Him. I hadn't even thought about that up until then. When Ben opened his eyes, he testified that angels were all around him playing musical instruments and singing. It was such a blessing to us all.

I had been christened as a child in the Presbyterian Church and confirmed in the Catholic Church. I was invited to a baptism that was taking place in the home pool of Paul Hair, who was pastoring the Interfellowship. I was standing on the edge of the pool watching a person being baptised. I had been sprinkled on the head as a child, but these people were being dipped backward into the pool and coming up changed people. I desperately wanted the same. It felt like that would put the icing on the cake for me, but I was only a guest, so I didn't say anything.

Paul Hair said that being baptised in the water symbolises Jesus' dying on the cross, immersing in the water symbolises Jesus being buried in the tomb, and being raised from the water symbolises Jesus rising from the dead. When we go down in the waters, we bury the 'old life' for good. That means the 'old life' is dead and buried, never to return. When we rise from the water we walk in a 'new life.' It was all extremely exciting, and I was busting to be baptised.

Then after the last person came up out of the waters, Paul said, "Is there anyone else?" That was all I needed. I said, "Yes. Me," and I jumped into the pool, high heels, clothes and all, and was baptised right there and then.

The scripture above clearly states we are to baptise others. It's not just for the pastor, minister, vicar or priest of a church. Once back in Christchurch I was asked if I would temporarily house a young couple with two children; both parents had recently been released from prison and needed temporary accommodation. At that time, we had a big house, so I was happy to oblige. We always prayed together as a family every night and the couple got involved. The dad had been addicted to drugs and was going through treatment.

I didn't have a lot to decorate my house with, but I did have posters and scriptures about God all over the place. I had randomly put posters up around the house and the one I put on the back of the toilet door, said, *O taste and see that the Lord is good; blessed is the man who trusts in Him.* —Psalm 34:8. One night, the dad met God. He had read the scripture while on the toilet and the words struck him. He had an experience with God that not only changed his life but removed his drug addiction. Instead of tasting drugs, he was now tasting God.

After his experience, there was a lot of excitement in the house. He and his wife wanted to be baptised. I did not know where there was a pool, so we decided right there and then to fill up the bath and baptise them there. That was a great day!

the invisible sentence

nine

it is also blessed to receive

I have shown you in all things, that by working hard in this way we must help the weak, remembering the words that the Lord Jesus himself said, "There is more happiness in giving than in receiving."

Acts 20:35

In the main, we lived off the benefit and charity. Living on the benefit meant that we went without most things. We lived out of the second-hand shops and watched out for the specials at the supermarket. I can remember sending my daughter to school once in a new school uniform that had fewer holes in it than the previous one. I heard later from people connected to the school about how a teacher had a child come into school to show off her new school uniform and it was full of holes. And I knew that was my daughter. But we just could not afford new school uniforms. During my whole journey I had to find and pay for 16 school uniforms. One blessing is that Lisa and her friends did not wear shoes to school when living in Whangaparaoa so I missed out on purchasing three shoe sizes.

I didn't even know there was such a thing as community support and that I could get help. I didn't know there were services in the community and funding for those in need. I didn't know I could get respite care or funding for school uniforms. I never had any time out because I didn't know it was there.

We never had holidays. Holidays were never a thought.

My husband was great. He never asked for money and I never put money into his prisoners' trust account as other families did.

I hated my trips to the supermarket. I would often have to put staples back as I just did not have enough to pay for them. If I had a bag of flour and yeast, we could make food. Lisa and I often laughed that we would write a book someday called '101 Recipes using Flour and Water'.

Jacqui was running up huge phone bills with her friends in Oamaru because it was important to her to stay connected with the people who loved and supported her and the phone company could not stop them.

If I had a bag of flour and yeast, we could make food. Lisa and I often laughed that we would write a book someday called '101 Recipes using Flour and Water'.

Costs for toll calls were exorbitant, several hundred dollars a month. I needed to keep phone contact with my husband so needed a phone and was frugal managing my money. I had learned to manage money well and it was never wasted.

We used to get fruit off the trees of the holiday homes, and I used to keep $2 aside to buy horse carrots, which was a big sack of carrots fit for animals and would go through the bag and pick out the good ones; and I grew my own greens in garden pots. We could never afford meat; cheese and sprouts were our main source of protein. But we never went without.

Jacqui worked at the local fish and chip shop at that time. The manager would send her home with the bits and pieces of fish left over from the day for the cat and we would cook it up for us. It was a real treat. The cat got no fish.

I would go pipi hunting down at the beach. I also would make my own bread daily. The neighbours would wake up to the sweet-smelling aroma of freshly baked bread so I was called the Health Lady. Little did they know it was not a matter of health at the time, it was a matter of survival.

But, in saying all this, people were generous. For a while I kept a notebook of what people had given me along with a plan to return the money when I could.

Once when I was offered a food parcel, I was worried about how I could pay it back. I now owed a lot of people and the bill was getting into the hundreds of dollars. I couldn't take any more charity. I told the social worker that I couldn't take it as I couldn't pay it back, that I owed too many people already.

We could never afford meat; cheese and sprouts were our main source of protein. But we never went without.

He said, "What do you mean." So, I told him about the notebook. This incredibly wise man said, "Throw it away!"

He said, "Well Verna, what's charity; in the Biblical sense?" I said, "Aw love," and he said, "Well, that is why they do it because it is through love. There is no way anyone will ever want their money back." He said, "You do not owe anyone anything. Throw the book away." So, I threw it away. What a relief. I felt a real sense of freedom. I didn't need to worry about that anymore.

My grandmother, who once gave me $20, reminded me that one day I would have my time of giving. She said, "All I want from you is to promise me that you will give back in some way some day when it is your turn to give."

Jesus reminded me that he had paid the debt for my sin when he died

the invisible sentence

for me. I did not owe Him anything, why should I owe these people?

Jesus said, "Without you receiving, they could not give, and I could not bless them. You are a blessing to them by receiving. Go and receive whenever I give."

ten

the food angels

This is why I tell you: do not be worried about the food and drink you need in order to stay alive, or about clothes for your body. After all, isn't life worth more than food? And isn't the body worth more than clothes? Look at the birds—they do not plant seeds, gather a harvest and put it into barns; yet your Father in heaven takes care of them! Aren't you worth much more than birds? Can any of you live a bit longer by worrying about it? And why worry about clothes? Look how the wildflowers grow: they do not work or make clothes for themselves. But I tell you that not even King Solomon with all his wealth had clothes as beautiful as one of these flowers. It is God who clothes the wild grass; grass that is here today and gone tomorrow, burned up in the oven. Won't he be all the more sure to clothe you? What little faith you have! So do not start worrying, 'Where will my food come from? Or my drink? or my clothes' (These are the things the pagans are always concerned about). Your Father in Heaven knows that you need all these things. Instead, be concerned about everything else with the Kingdom of God and with what he requires of you, and he will provide you with all these other things. So do not worry about tomorrow; it will have worries of its own. There is no need to add to the troubles each day brings.

Matthew 6:25-34

When the benefit and the charity money ran out, God's miraculous provision always stepped in, and this is interesting because all I held onto was this scripture and its promise by God. It is headed up in my Bible, 'Do Not Worry'.

I knew I was in God's will. All He required of me was to bring up my children and visit my husband in prison and focus on that. So, then He had to step in and provide for our every need and He did. I had some miraculous provisions from finding houses, to water provision, petrol, and food.

One evening we had no food, not even flour. I was sitting at the table and there was nothing in the cupboards and I told the children to set the table for tea. We all said grace and thanked God for our meal. We'd got quite cocky with God. He always met our needs, and He was so good to us, but this was something quite different. This was a real leap of faith. I thought, *'Okay, this is God's problem not mine, and I was seeking His kingdom and so He will provide me with all these other things. We have courage in God's presence, because we are sure that he hears us if we ask him for anything that is according to his will. He hears us whenever we ask Him; and since we know that this is true, we know also that He gives us what we asked from Him.'* — 1 John 5:14-15.

As we finished grace, there was a knock at the door and a woman was standing there with a big bag of groceries and I can remember distinctly there were Coco Pops in there, something we never had. She said to me, "I have just come from the Whangaparaoa supermarket and God spoke

the food angels

to me." Of course by then I understood that God did speak to people. "He told me to put two of everything in the trolley and gave me your name and address, and told me to bring it to you."

So, there she was standing at the front door holding our tea and breakfast for the next day.

By then I was I frequenting church meetings in the area but had never met this woman, nor did I ever see her again.

I believe to this day that I had a radical encounter with an angel appearing in physical form. Hebrews 13:2 says, *"Remember to welcome strangers in your homes. There were some who did that and welcomed angels without knowing it."*

The owner brought over my coffee and then she said, "Do you have small children at home?" I thought this a very odd question, but I said "Yes." She then said, "Do you want to take some food home for them?"

Then there was the time, after visiting Paul in prison. I had 50 cents left in my purse.

I was exhausted after my seven kilometre walk back from the prison to Albany and I thought, *'Blow it, I am going to shout myself to a cup of coffee.'*

I went into the coffee shop. It was around 3.30pm and the place was busy. I ordered a coffee and seated myself at the back of the shop. I was feeling rather guilty that the 50 cents could have been spent on other things and I was watching the people come and go with their coffees, along with their idle chatter.

The owner brought over my coffee and then she said, "Do you have small children at home?" I thought this a very odd question, but I said "Yes."

"Do you want to take some food home for them?" she said. I never prompted anything and I never asked. I was just sitting in the corner with my coffee minding my own business and I said, "Yes, I would love that."

She came back with a cardboard box and said, "Help yourself." I did not know where to start. I cautiously lifted the perspex covers protecting the food and slipped a few sandwiches into the box. Then she came back and said, "Take some more." So, I doubled my lot and took a few more sandwiches and slipped in a cake each for the children.

By now I was thinking all my Christmases had come at once. There was enough food for one day in the box and I was ecstatic. Then she came back again and said loudly, "TAKE THE LOT!" I then proceeded to fill the box to the brim with pies, sausage rolls, buns, and everything imaginable that we would never have been able to afford. I cleaned out that shop. I had enough food to last us five days—breakfast, dinner and tea.

Then there was the water. I was living in a duplex near the beach. We were living in an area that relied on tank water and if the water ran out you had to buy it in. When it rained, I bathed the children and washed the bedding. That ensured we would always keep our tank full.

Summer came and there was a drought. My tank was getting rather empty and we were running out of water fast. I asked God to provide our water and I believed He would.

Next day I expected rain but, to the contrary, it was a gorgeous sunny day. I was angry with God about this, as I thought He had let me down.

Then later in the day I received a phone call from my landlord who lived in Auckland. He said, "I have been thinking about you today and

the food angels

that your tank water must be getting pretty low." I said, "Actually, I've got no water, my tank has run dry." He said, "No problem. If you have a long hose you can syphon water from our tank into yours. Help yourself."

Well strangely enough, I did have a long hose. It was large in diameter about 10mm wide and 50m long. I had carried it with me on all my travels right from Oamaru. It had been used on the farm and I had never really thought about why I even had it. But there it was and, yes, my tank was instantly filled.

the invisible sentence

eleven

God, my heavenly husband and father

Your Creator will be like a husband to you—the Lord Almighty is His name. The holy God of Israel will save you—He is the ruler of the world.

Isaiah 54:5

It was not easy living without my husband. There were times I got quite despondent that I did not have a physical husband in the house. I had to learn new skills like changing a light bulb, moving to a new house on my own and coping with any emergencies.

I had been given a jar of jam and I could not get the lid off. I remembered how my dad used to put the lid in the door hinge and try to unscrew it that way, but this was just not working. This was the last straw. I just burst into tears. Next thing I hear God's voice, "Run it under the hot tap." I hadn't thought of that and had never been shown that way, but I did, and the lid came off instantly.

I first witnessed the amazing healing power of Jesus when Kate got sick with a life-threatening chest infection and needed a doctor urgently.

We had just moved to another house in a new area and had not even unpacked. The phone had not been connected, and I had not organised a doctor. I had no car and knew no one. It was 3.00am. The baby was extremely sick. I knew I needed to get urgent medical attention for her. But I didn't know where I could find a doctor or even where a hospital was. I had no one to turn to. That is when God stepped in as my husband.

I had heard about God's miraculous healing powers in the book of Acts in the Bible. I didn't know that God healed today, but I am a rational thinker and knowing I had an exciting relationship with the living God, surmised that what He did then, He could still do today.

So, for that extremely sick baby lying in her bed, I did what Peter the Apostle did. I laid hands on her chest and said, "Be healed in Jesus' name."

In an instant, I saw the power of God enter my baby and centre on her lungs. They were just glowing, and the power seared her lungs like a hot iron. As quickly as the power came, it left, leaving my baby instantly healed and well.

That same baby at two years old was very mischievous and at times I worried for her life.

I had built a fence on my property to keep her in which made my house resemble the local prison, but she would climb the neighbour's fence and just swing around it to break out.

I needed eyes in the back of my head to keep her safe. I couldn't even turn my back for a moment, for in a blink of eye, she would be gone. There were a few times when I had called the neighbourhood search party out to look for her when I couldn't find her. But God always kept her safe.

One day it was pouring with rain and once again she got out. She had managed to cross the road in front of our house and onto the adjacent park, her little feet running as fast as they could go. She was extremely

God, my heavenly husband and father

fast, and I just couldn't catch her. As I ran, my skirt was catching in the mud and it became heavy and weighed down. As a result, I was slipping over and falling to the ground. Ahead was a busy road and I knew if I did not get to her before then it would be all over.

I was frantic. My only hope was that God would intervene. From deep within me I called out to God, "Help."

At that precise moment God summoned five seagulls. They flew up from the beach if on a mission. All I could do was stop and watch. Flying in unison they appeared as bomber aircraft seeking out their target. They came to my daughter and flew all around her stopping her in her tracks. They perched on her head and danced around her. She tried to catch each one and as she reached out, they would dart away, just in time.

It was a total relief being able to catch up with her and to gather her safely into my arms. Then the seagulls went on their way as if nothing had happened.

As Kate grew older, she would stay with my parents for holidays. I used to put her on the train in Christchurch and my mother would pick her up in Oamaru. One day, after seeing her off from the railway station I was driving home and I heard the voice of Satan saying in a guttural voice, "Your daughter will die."

One day, after seeing her off from the railway station I was driving home and I heard the voice of Satan saying in a guttural voice, "Your daughter will die."

Now this is one voice that has no credence in my life. I reminded him that, *she will not die; instead she will live and proclaim what the Lord has done* –Psalm 118:17 and, *the thief comes in order to steal, kill, and destroy. I (Jesus) have come in order that you might have life—life in all its fullness* –John 10:10. I believe that the power of these scriptures overrode what was about to unfold.

That evening, on the television, there was breaking news. I heard that the passenger train to Oamaru had been derailed in Timaru. A grain silo had spilled open as the train was passing and engulfed one of the carriages. They were waiting to hear if passengers had been injured or were dead. I knew that was the train my daughter was on. Inside myself I had confidence that my daughter was okay.

I got a phone call from my mum. As it turned out the grain had engulfed the carriage right behind where Kate was sitting. No one was hurt as there were no passengers in that carriage. I believe that the devil had purposed her demise, but she was okay.

Early in my walk, I was concerned about Paul's salvation and just how far Christ would go to accept a person. I knew kidnapping was directly forbidden in the Hebrew law (Exodus 21:16; Deuteronomy 24:7) and was made punishable by death.

One night, God the Father took me into the great throne room in Heaven. He was seated on His throne amid the white bright cloud I had seen when I had first met Him on earth, and I found myself sitting on his knee. I stepped up and cuddled into him like a small child. I felt so secure and safe. He had His big Bible sitting on a small ornate-looking table to the left of Him. He picked it up and opened it in a very reverential manner. It spread right across me and the robe on His knees. This Bible was different from what I had seen on Earth. It had big, very black writing. He opened it at 1 Timothy, and we read the whole chapter together. But what stood out for me was 1 Timothy 1:9-11. *It must be remembered, of course, that laws are made, not for good people, but for lawbreakers* and criminals, for the godless and sinful, for those that are not religious or spiritual, for those that kill their fathers and mothers, for murderers, for the immoral, for sexual perverts, for kidnappers, for those who lie and give false testimony or who do anything else contrary to sound doctrine.

I had the realisation then that Jesus died for the whole world because of His great love for all of us. That included kidnappers, and every person who has ever perpetrated a hurtful, destructive, dishonest or unloving act … everyone!

And He reminded me that I was saved by grace and grace alone and by nothing I had done or could ever do, even though I was a sinner, and had done it ignorantly in unbelief. And, on top of that, He had a purpose for my life and what is exciting is that He is using me as a pattern to others who are going to believe in Him for everlasting life.

1 Timothy 1:12-16, *I give thanks to Christ Jesus our Lord, who has given me strength for my work. I thank Him for considering me worthy and appointing me to serve Him, even though in the past I spoke evil of Him and persecuted and insulted Him. But God was merciful to me because I did not yet have faith and did not know what I was doing. And our Lord poured out His abundant grace on me and gave me the faith and love which are ours in union with Christ Jesus. This is a true saying, to be completely accepted and believed—Christ Jesus came into the world to save sinners. I am the worst of them but God was merciful to me in order that Christ Jesus might show his full patience in dealing with*

I had the realisation then that Jesus died for the whole world because of His great love for all of us. That included kidnappers, and every person who has ever perpetrated a hurtful, destructive, dishonest or unloving act … everyone!

me, the worst of sinners, as an example (pattern) of all those who would later believe in him and receive eternal life.

So, God is using me as an example or pattern? I was quite taken with that. This was a huge responsibility, but I was extremely proud that He had chosen me.

I can remember my mother using patterns to make my dresses when I was young. She would use the same ones over and over again. They would come in a large envelope and they would be made of tissue paper, which was incredibly soft and fragile. They would come with specific instructions about how to place them on the fabric and how to cut around them so that, once sewn, they would fit to size. There were many different pieces, and she would pin them onto the fabric then cut around them.

On the fabric, there is a line called the grain line, which runs parallel with the grain of the fabric. She would use a tape measure to measure from the grain line to ensure the paper pattern was in the right position.

There were notches in the pattern and these were marked onto the fabric by cutting an extra section out of the fabric to avoid cutting into the seam allowance.

Once the pattern was cut out, all the pieces were sewn together placing the notches of one piece up against another piece and sewing it together.

These pieces looked nothing like the finished article. It was only with great sewing precision that the finished article would end up as a perfect dress.

The Old Testament declares that there is a pattern for the work of God's people that was given as an instruction about how things were to be made or take place.

Patterns were given to Noah to build the Ark, Moses to build the tabernacle and to Joshua about how to conquer the city of Jericho. But God said I am a pattern too. I wondered how God was going to put all my pieces together with great precision to produce something wonderful out of me. I pondered, *'What could that be?'*

twelve

giving up smoking

*Jesus looked straight at them and answered,
"This is impossible for human beings,
but for God everything is possible."*

Matthew 19:26

I was a cigarette smoker and totally addicted. I could not even answer the phone without lighting up. When we owned the pizza parlour, I had access to cigarettes whenever I needed them but now, on the benefit, I couldn't afford such luxuries. To satisfy my addiction I would buy a small pouch of tobacco and would sit at my kitchen table and roll the whole pouch up in advance, really small, so it would last the two weeks before my next benefit payment. I would work out my daily intake and spread that over the whole day. I had read that my body is the temple of the Holy Spirit and I hated that I just could not break the habit. I didn't have the will power to give up. I always had an excuse, and it was always a 'poor me' excuse like you deserve a cigarette because of what you are going through, you need them right now or, just one more will not hurt.

I had talked to God about it, but I just could not overcome this horrible habit, which I felt I had to break on my own. I talked to Margaret about it and she was just lovely and said that God will deal with it when I was ready and not to worry about it. I wanted to be ready now, but it was just insurmountable. I was forever spraying myself with perfume and using mouthwash but, even then, I would go to church with my hair smelling of tobacco. I felt everyone knew I smoked. I did not know of any other Christian who smoked but assumed, like me, we all kept it a secret.

Then one day when I was at the Hibiscus Coast Inter-fellowship, there was a word of knowledge that someone had a cloud over their lungs. I knew immediately that was me. I was called up to the front for prayer to get rid of the smoking. I didn't know that God could do such a thing. I had not heard about deliverance and never equated smoking to a demon or to any scripture in the Bible except where Jesus cast demons out of a man and into some pigs.

Once up the front I said, "Would God do that for me?" and a woman said, "You had better believe it lady," and she laughed. Before I even had hands laid on me, the power of God hit me and I fell to the floor. I saw this animal in the spirit with a big fluffy tail going round and round inside of me. It was like it had been caught out, that its time was up, and it had nowhere to run. Then the pastor called out the spirit of nicotine and this animal came up and out of my mouth. I then saw into the sky (even though there was a roof on the building) and this animal ascending way, way up into the heavens.

Margaret told me later that I made such a noise like I was vomiting it up all over the floor. I am grateful God in His grace spared me from knowing that.

giving up smoking

Unfortunately, I was smoking three days later after the deliverance. I felt so guilty I had let the Lord and myself down. It wasn't until several years later that God broached me again on the subject. I was praying one night, and I distinctly heard the Lord say, "Go and get a chest x-ray Verna." I thought, this is it. I've now got cancer just because I have been disobedient on this matter. So there and then I said to the Lord (silly me), "Okay, I will give up until I get the results of the chest x-ray."

I had to think about what to tell the doctor, so I went to the doctor and just said, "God has told me to come and ask for a chest x-ray."

> **I was praying one night, and I distinctly heard the Lord say, "Go and get a chest x-ray Verna."**

Interestingly, at that time, the doctor was also a smoker. He had an ashtray on his desk in the surgery. It was before smoking was regarded as a medical hazard. He never said a word, he just wrote me out a referral and told me to contact the hospital.

I immediately went home and phoned for an appointment. It was in three days' time. I thought to myself, *'Okay, that's three days I won't smoke. I can get through three days.'*

I went to the appointment and had the chest x-ray. They said they would contact me and the doctor in the next few days with the results. Surely, I could last another two days without a smoke.

Two days came and went, then a week came and went. I rang the hospital about the results, and they couldn't find any record of them. I could not get another appointment for a further x-ray for at least another two weeks. They said they would look for the records in the meantime. I remembered I had promised God I would not smoke until I had got my results and I was honouring that.

One month later the results arrived. My chest x-ray showed that I was clear. God had held up the results and His grace had stepped in and I hadn't had a cigarette for one month. I now felt I was in control and decided that no matter what was going on in my head about poor me and have a cigarette, all I had to remember was DO NOT PUT A CIGARETTE TO YOUR LIPS.

Since that day in 1990 I have not touched a cigarette.

thirteen

God moves the heavens

Seek your happiness in the Lord,
and He will give you your heart's desire.

Psalm 37:4

When I was a young girl, I was infatuated with Halley's Comet. I wanted to be an astronomer when I grew up and study the comet. I was drawn to books about it and I would cut pictures out of magazines. I made it my business to know everything there was to know about this famous celestial object. There was something intriguing about its brightness and awe that captivated me. It visited the earth every 76 years and last came in 1910.

As a six-year-old, I had worked out that it would be 26 years before it would revisit the earth and I would be 32. I decided that I would be there for that as a priority.

I was living in Orewa at the time and the night that Halley's Comet was to arrive I was packing a removal truck to take our furniture back to Christchurch. Paul had served 18 months in Paremoremo maximum-security and had been reclassified as medium security risk, so was sent back to Paparua Prison in Christchurch.

The newspapers were full about the return of Halley's Comet and it was predicted that the best sighting would be in my old hometown of Oamaru. People from all over the world had descended on the small town with their big optical reflecting telescopes all ready for the viewing.

I was angry at God who I felt was 'throwing it back in my face' since the best sighting was predicted to be in Oamaru, and I was as far away from Oamaru as I could be.

Once the removal truck had left, I piled the children into my 120Y Datsun car ready for the long drive down the country from Orewa back to Christchurch. A lovely caring couple in the church were concerned about me and had booked and paid for a motel at Turangi, a six-hour drive from Orewa, for us to stay the night. In their words, "We want you to have a good night's rest and a good meal before you embark on your next day, and please phone in when you get there so we know you are safe."

We arrived at the motel in Turangi. The accommodation was amazing. It had hot pools and our unit was extravagant. I forgot about Halley's Comet as I became absorbed in the children's needs. Tomorrow would be a big day.

At 2.30 am God woke me, "Wake up, wake up Verna. Pull back the curtains."

We settled in for the night and all went to sleep quickly. At 2.30am God woke me, "Wake up, wake up Verna. Pull back the curtains." And there it was, Halley's Comet in all its splendour, flying like a celestial kite, but remaining motionless, flanked by two hills set in a valley, its heart big and aglow and its tail, although rather short, streaming. I couldn't believe my eyes. I woke the children and we watched it for several hours.

Next day the news media was full of the Halley's Comet sighting; or lack of it.

In Mt Albert, Auckland, thousands had turned out for the appearance paying $2 to the Lions Club for a chance to peer at the heavens. What they saw was no way near as spectacular as what was expected. It was described in the media as a 'little puff of smoke' or a 'faint fuzzy ball.' In Auckland, the biggest telescope in town brought in people at $5 a time. For those who saw the comet in 1910 said it did not compare anything with the last sighting.

The New York Times reported, "The consensus is in. Halley's Comet was a fizzle. The celebrated once-in-a-lifetime visitor from space, which triggered mass hysteria in 1910 and mass merchandising in 1986, surprised astronomers last week by fading and losing most of its tail just as it was making its closest approach to earth. It appeared small, fuzzy, and feeble."

For the millions who purchased binoculars and telescopes for the historic visit, stood outside in their pyjamas or travelled thousands of miles for a clear vantage point they were left disappointed with the wispy blob of light. Observers commented that the visitation was a dud.

The Oamaru siting had also been a huge disappointment. It was cloudy and there was no sighting. But the best sighting was, guess where, Turangi, and we had front row seats.

the invisible sentence

fourteen

one day left —then homeless!

If you believe, you will receive whatever you ask for in prayer.

Matthew 21:22

When we got back to Christchurch, we stayed with my aunt and began house hunting. Once again, there was no rental accommodation available. We looked everywhere throughout Christchurch, to no avail.

Then one day after coming back from visiting Paul at the prison, I'd had enough. I pulled out the phone directory and randomly picked a land agent who happened to be Harcourts in South Brighton, a suburb of Christchurch. I phoned them up and asked if they had any permanent housing for rent?

They said, "No, we have nothing long term at all, but we do have a temporary one." Then I thought, *'Temporary is better than nothing.'*

"It is only for three months. You can have it, maybe, if the landlord approves of you. The landlord lives in Whangaparaoa in the North Island," he said.

"That's a coincidence, I have just come from there, who are the landlords?" I said.

He named them and they happened to be my neighbours when I lived in the first house and I knew them very well. I got on the phone and asked them why hadn't they told me about their house? They said, "We knew you wanted permanent accommodation and we didn't want to disappoint you by moving you out when it was time to be sold," but they said, "If you want the house you are welcome to it."

It was a four-bedroom home perfect for our needs. The other great blessing that came out of the house was I got a little job transporting the landlord's elderly father to visit his wife in hospital each day.

Twenty minutes later he arrived in his big flash car. I felt like the red carpet had been laid out for me. The vicar was both ecstatic and visibly shaken at what he had just witnessed.

Eventually, the house did sell, and we moved in with a girlfriend who lived down the road, whose husband was also in prison. From there we moved out to the south side of Christchurch and lived in a missionary's house while they were on the mission field. We were there for nine months and my father-in-law, Reg, joined us.

The local Anglican vicar was the stand-in landlord, and we got to know him well. Two weeks out from the missionary's return home, he came around and told us that we had two weeks to be out of the house. The missionary couple were arriving home on the Saturday.

The vicar regularly visited to see how we were progressing with our house hunting.

"Have you got a house yet?" he would politely enquire.

"Yes we have," I would say.

"Where is it?" He would say… and I would say, "God has not shown us yet."

He rightly appeared quite perturbed. He had the responsibility of ensuring that we were out and the missionaries got their house back. On the Friday before the Saturday when the missionaries were to return, the house we were to move to, had still not been revealed to us, but we packed all our gear anyway and set up the cardboard boxes in the rooms, ready for the move.

It was about midday on the Friday. The vicar arrived, and we were sitting on our boxes. He looked relieved when he saw the boxes and the furniture stacked up. He said, "I see you are moving, where are you going?" Before I could answer, the phone rang. It was the manager of Housing New Zealand. I had gone there previously to ask for a house, but we couldn't get one because we didn't have enough points to fit their eligibility criteria.

He said, "We have a desperate situation on our hands. We have had some street kids come in and occupy one of our larger houses and we need to get them out. We need a family to move in straight away so they can't return. We have a note on a file that you were needing to move by today. Have you got a house yet? Can you move today? We need someone in there urgently, today."

The following Sunday, the vicar preached to his church on faith and trusting God using our testimony of how God always provides.

And of course, I said, "Yes. We'll take it." He said that he would come out personally to take me and show me the house. Twenty minutes later he arrived in his big flash car. I felt like the red carpet had been laid out for me. The vicar was both ecstatic and visibly shaken at what he had just witnessed.

The house was the largest Housing New Zealand property in Christchurch with six large bedrooms, two lounges and a kitchen. It was so big it had two power metres.

"If you take it today, we will give you a three-month rent holiday because we need it occupied now," he said.

So, we packed up the trailer and moved in ourselves. By then we were so used to moving, we would often laugh that we had become a removal company and called ourselves McFelin & McFelin Removals.

I heard later, that on the following Sunday, the vicar preached to his church on faith and trusting God using our testimony of how God always provides.

fifteen

ruling and reigning

You plotted evil against me, but God turned it into good, in order to preserve the lives of many people who are alive today because of what happened.

Genesis 50:20

My first open vision of a demon as an adult appeared, strangely enough, at a prayer meeting. We were all praising God and lifting our hands to Him, but my spirit was telling me something was radically wrong. Even though this was a prayer meeting I sensed a real darkness in the room. Next thing, I came eye to eye with a large demonic being. It was similar to the ones I had met that shook my bed violently when I was a child. This one was about 2.1 metres tall, white, with open sores, dressed in a bright green outfit with a big black cape. I distinctly knew immediately it was a religious spirit. It was standing just outside of the circle we had formed, holding its cape over the people. We looked at each other, then it blinked as it realised, I had caught it out. Then, when I looked again it was gone. I pondered the experience for a few weeks wondering what to do about it and thought I'd better report it to the church authorities. I hadn't known at the time that I had power over it and could cast it out. The authorities were not impressed and would not accept it and said I had brought it in from when I visited the prison. I then remembered the scripture, *"Listen! I am sending you out just like sheep to a pack of wolves. You must be as cautious as snakes and gentle as doves,"* —Matthew 10:16.

There are just some things that God shows us that we just don't share. It's about ruling as a righteous person and remembering that the ultimate calling is to love, not judge, no matter what.

One lovely still night, I was lying on my bunk bed. I slept on the top and I could poke my head out the window to look at the stars. As I looked out that night, the Lord was talking to me about each of the stars and constellations, naming them one by one. Then I had a check in my spirit that something was not right. Was this really God talking to me? I decided it was not. I pulled my head back inside and saw Jesus standing in the corner of the room as He had done when I was five. But was this really Jesus? My spirit was saying otherwise.

> **As I resigned to the fact that it was not God speaking to me, at that moment, I was attacked by beings in Centurion armour just like the two I had met when I was a baby in my cot, their helmets almost touched the ceiling. But this time, they were dark beings, not the transparent ones.**

As I resigned to the fact that it was not God speaking to me, at that moment, I was attacked by beings in Centurion armour just like the two I had met when I was a baby in my cot, their helmets almost touched the ceiling. But this time, they were dark beings, not the transparent ones.

I got up and went into the lounge and there were about thirty of these things crammed into the room, all attacking me.

I said to Jesus, "But I put the blood of Jesus over the house before I went to bed to protect us. Why are they here?"

God said, "But you didn't cast out what was not of Me."

Then it was full on. Their helmets would hit my head and sparks would fly off. This cut off my thinking and paralysed me so all I could do was say, "Praise God, Praise God."

Even though they were attacking me, I felt I was in an impenetrable bubble with God completely protecting me. I knew that they could not harm me no matter how hard they tried, and I also knew I was going to be in for an awfully long night. I had never cast out demons before, but I knew God was in his praises so, if I kept praising God, maybe they would just go away.

I did know that Jesus had given me the assurance that *He has given me the power to overcome all the power of the enemy and nothing shall harm me* –Luke 10:19. I was about to learn a very big lesson. Sometimes God puts the Goliath on your path for you to find the David within you.

As I praised God, they would begin to leave. It took me eight hours to clear the room and the last one to leave was Fear.

When it left, I was shaking all over and exhausted, but I knew that I had stepped into a new realm of authority that night. I knew I had power over the enemy and after that experience nothing could faze me. What Satan had intended for evil, God had turned into good. Satan had done me one great big favour.

Not long after that experience I was doing the dishes one night and was quite tired from my day. Lisa had her friend Cheri around, and they were having a sleepover. They burst into the kitchen and said they wanted to make popcorn. All I could think of was the mess I was going to have to clean up afterward.

> **I was about to learn a very big lesson. Sometimes God puts the Goliath on your path for you to find the David within you.**

the invisible sentence

Then God spoke to me and said, "Lay hands on the girls." I thought, how do I explain this one? So, I said to them both, "How would you like to know the real love of the Lord," to which they both said, "Yes."

We went into the lounge. I had dirty washing piled everywhere and the room was a mess. I had planned to clean it all up in the morning. I laid hands on the girls and they both fell under the power of God into the piles of dirty washing and mess. Cheri had a healing of memories. God took her back to when she was in the womb. Her mother later confirmed what she saw. Cheri was completely healed. Lisa found herself in a vision at the foot of the cross along with Mary, the mother of God. Jesus was calling her to Him. Then she had a vision of a motor vehicle accident involving a red and blue car. She explained the scene even down to a brick wall and an ash can. We immediately all prayed that the occupants would be safe. It was like a burden we were carrying. We kept praying until that lifted. I found tongues so useful for this type of prayer.

> **I laid hands on the girls and they both fell under the power of God into the piles of dirty washing and mess. Cheri had a healing of memories. God took her back to when she was in the womb. Her mother later confirmed what she saw.**

The next day we went to the beach. Lisa and Cheri were still excited about what had happened the night before and told all their friends about the experience. They all were enthralled and just as they finished talking, we looked back at the road and there was the red and blue car being towed by. Everyone cheered. In the newspaper that night it stated that it was a miracle that no one was injured.

I often laugh how God visited us amid our mess and dirty washing that night.

When we arrived back in Christchurch after living in Orewa, I attended the local Catholic church. I so missed the Hibiscus Coast Interfellowship. I felt so spiritually dry. With the support of the church, I started a Bible study group that met weekly. But I hated it… it was so boring. No one appeared to know God like I did, but they were all incredibly open. I was hoping God would show up, but He never seemed to.

One day I'd had enough and I said to God, "I might as well be with my friend down the road praying for these people rather than be here. If You don't show up today, I'm stopping the meeting."

That morning, everyone arrived as usual, including the priest. This time things went a bit differently. Rather than the priest rushing into opening in prayer as he had done every other time, he quietly waited. I distinctly felt the Holy Spirit walk into the room and I had a feeling of real anticipation.

Then God orchestrated the removal of my two children from the room. They left together for no apparent reason. Then the priest poised himself to open in prayer. But what I saw was that what he was trying to say was just not coming out of his mouth. He could not speak. Then God spoke through him and said, "May we see Your kingdom reign among us."

The priest obviously wasn't expecting that and he took a deep gasp, and I could see that he was taken aback about what had just happened. He tried to take control of himself and pray again, then he opened his mouth and God said, "On earth."

> **No one appeared to know God like I did, but they were all incredibly open. I was hoping God would show up, but He never seemed to…**

The meeting was just the same as before but when it finished the priest couldn't get away from our house quickly enough. It was customary that we always waved off our visitors, so I went out to the gate to see him off.

the invisible sentence

He got into his car and ended up grating the gears all the way up the street.

The next Sunday at Mass, the priest was more devout than usual. You could see he'd had an experience that was inexplicable, and he knew that it was God. It was many months later that I told him that I knew God had spoken through him.

At that time we were moving once again, and he had supported me by storing our furniture at his place. I have often thought how God used me that day and used my furniture for the next six months to remind him that God is real even outside of the Mass.

Not only did I visit my husband weekly in prison, but I also occasionally visited my sister-in-law at the Christchurch Women's Prison. One time she talked about how the women were sewing clothes for their children and asked if we would do a collection of material in the community as they could not afford to purchase it. I put a word out to the local churches in the area. The Presbyterian church at Hornby had made a large collection and phoned me to say I could come and collect it.

I have often thought how God used me that day and used my furniture for the next six months to remind him that God is real even outside of the Mass.

I arrived on the manse doorstep and when the minister opened the door, he prophesied over me. I was not expecting that. He said, "You will be working very closely with the Māori people." I thought this was very possible because I had met so many in prison and I had friends who were Māori, but God was to reveal the extent of this much later.

I took the material home and we decided to pray over the pieces. The scriptures say in Acts 19:11-12, *God was performing unusual miracles through Paul. Even handkerchiefs and aprons he had used were taken to the sick, and their diseases were driven away, and the evil spirits would go out of them.*

So, we prayed over each piece before we sent the material into the prison. We never saw the results of these prayers, but I did see the results from the time I prayed over hankies when my dad was sick in hospital. He had been hospitalised with an unknown illness that had affected his mind. I went to Oamaru to support my mother so we could be together by his side.

> **I knew though that the hankies containing God's power had touched my dad.**

The hospital did various tests and could not get to the bottom of the problem. I decided to pray over all his hankies in the hospital room. My mother was there, and she had never heard me pray in tongues. I was returning to Christchurch the next day and I told Mum to make sure he had a hanky on him at any given time, and she did.

The following week I went back to Oamaru and when I went into my father's hospital room, he was waving his arms in the air worshipping. He told me that he had met 'Verna's God'.

"But he's your God too, Dad…" to which he said, "No, I met Verna's God last night. I thought I was leaving the hospital in a box, but now I am okay."

I felt quite unsettled he had called God, 'Verna's God'. And then I remembered that in the Old Testament, God was referred to as the God of Isaac, Abraham and Jacob so I then thought it must be okay for Dad to call Him my God, so I never mentioned it again. I knew though that the hankies containing God's power had touched my dad.

the invisible sentence

sixteen

the adventures of intercession

On your walls Jerusalem, I have placed sentries (watchmen on the walls); They must never be silent day or night. They must remind the Lord of his promises and never let him forget them. They must give him no rest until he restores Jerusalem and makes it a city the whole world praises.

Isaiah 62:6-7

Now mortal man, I am making you a lookout (watchman on the wall) for the nation of Israel. You must pass onto them the warnings I give you.

Ezekiel 33:7

When I first began my prayer life, I spent many hours in prayer. I carried a notebook with the names of people I had met, and their needs, and I would pray over them daily. I took this responsibility very seriously.

I was a single mum with four children to care for and disciplined prayer was not easy. The book became larger and larger. My prayer life became a stress and a burden, but I really wanted to serve God, and this was one way I could do it.

One day God spoke to me and said, "Throw away the book. I will let you know what to pray for before it happens," and He gave me Isaiah 42:9, *The things I have predicted have now come true. Now I will tell you of new things even before they begin to happen.*

> **One day God spoke to me and said, "Throw away the book. I will let you know what to pray for before it happens,"**

The day I threw that book away was the day I experienced immense freedom in God and that was the day I embarked on a real prayer adventure. My relationship with God became stronger and I spent more hours in prayer than before, and it became an adventure and no longer a burden.

God would speak the names of people and their situations and I would pray for them. At times I had to warn people of imminent danger. That was when I became a 'watchman on the wall'.

In the Bible during Isaiah's time, the cities of the Middle East were fortified with walls surrounding them. People were set on top of these walls as lookouts. Their job was to keep a watchful eye out for the enemy who might attack without warning. These watchmen were the first lines of defence for the city.

In Matthew 13, God says that every believer has been given eyes to see and ears to hear. But a watchman must be equipped by God to see what others do not see and he or she has a unique capacity to see when the enemy is invading before anyone else. The enemy can come disguised, but a spiritual watchman is very alert so that the Body of Christ, family members and others can be quickly warned. It also involves care-taking the land and restraining natural disasters or evading man-made anthropogenic ones. It carries a huge responsibility as thousands of people may be reliant on the prayer and report of the watchman, and it could involve the safety of a city or a nation.

the adventures of intercession

As a watchman on the wall, I have learned to sleep with 'one eye open' because I am forever 'watching on the wall' and waiting on God's voice for that inevitable instruction. I learned that this is to 'pray unceasing'. It is always to be tuned into God, spiritually awake at every moment.

This is a very personal journey and most of my experiences I cannot share in this book or with anyone. It is between me and God. But I do know that God is totally reliant on the obedience of the watchman on the wall for Him to carry out His purposes on earth, because God will never override a person's will and because of this He wants many more of His people to intercede and commit to this calling. I later found out it is what people call intercession.

My first intercession experience was when God told me about a toddler who had climbed into a fishpond in Waikanae, just north of Wellington. The parents had been searching for the toddler and found him face down in the pond. God alerted me to this situation.

Holy Spirit and I prayed that the toddler would be found and that he would live. I prayed until I had a sense of peace that everything would be all right.

I told my friend about the experience and several weeks later there was a news item on Christian television about a child being rescued from drowning in a family fishpond in Waikanae. It was a Christian couple I didn't even know, and they don't know to this day that God intervened through the prayers of a single mum with a husband in prison who they didn't even know.

Another time, I got a phone call from a friend who said a child had fallen into a swimming pool and would I please pray. I asked God to save the child and He said, "No. The child is dead."

> **The parents had been searching for the toddler and found him face down in the pond. God alerted me to this situation.**

I argued with God about this, stating a case that this child had a life to live on earth and should not be called to Heaven right now. It was if I was presenting my case in the courts of Heaven for justice to prevail. I was ferocious in my Spirit stating my rights and hugely confident that I was right. I reminded God that I was one righteous person and of his conversation with Abraham about saving Sodom from destruction and how he would save Sodom if there were one righteous man living there. If the family had called for prayer for their child, then they too were obviously righteous.

> **I argued with God about this, stating a case that this child had a life to live on earth and should not be called to Heaven right now. It was if I was presenting my case in the courts of Heaven for justice to prevail.**

Then the two men left and went on toward Sodom, but the Lord remained with Abraham. Abraham approached the Lord and asked, "Are you really going to destroy the innocent with the guilty? If there are fifty innocent people in the city, will you destroy the whole city? Won't you spare it in order to save the fifty? Surely you won't kill the innocent with the guilty. That's impossible! You can't do that. If you did, the innocent would be punished along with the guilty. That is impossible. The judge of all the earth has to act justly." The Lord answered, "If I find fifty innocent people in Sodom, I will spare the whole city for their sake." Abraham spoke again, "Please forgive my boldness in continuing to speak to you, Lord. I am only a man and have no right to say anything. But perhaps there will be only forty-five innocent people instead of fifty. Will you destroy the whole city because there are five too few? The Lord answered, "I will not destroy the city if I find forty-five innocent people."

Abraham spoke again, "Perhaps there will be only forty." He replied, "I will not destroy it if there are forty." Abraham said, "Please don't be angry, Lord, but I must speak again. What if there are only thirty?" He said, "I will not do it if I find thirty."

Abraham said, "Please forgive my boldness in continuing to speak to you, Lord. Suppose that only twenty are found?" He said, "I will not destroy the city if I find twenty." Abraham said, "Please don't be angry, Lord, and I will speak only once more. What if only ten are found?"

He said, "I will not destroy it if there are ten." After he had finished speaking with Abraham, the Lord went away, and Abraham returned home, –Genesis 18:22-33.

Then God conceded and said, "Yes, you have your heart's desire, the child lives."

It was then, that I discovered I could change God's mind if I put up a convincing argument. Was this what the theologians call wrestling with God? Or was He going to save the child in the first place? Was He showing me how powerful, merciful and loving He really is? Does He enjoy having a good healthy argument with me?

Later in the day I got a phone call from my friend. I decided it was a good time to witness, so I got in first and said yes, God has told me that the child is alive to which she was amazed. I then explained the conversation I'd had with God. Later that week, I met the parents of the child and they were overawed and thankful that God had intervened. They had been church attendees but hadn't been going for some years. They decided that they would recommit their lives and return to church.

> **It was then, that I discovered I could change God's mind if I put up a convincing argument.**

I just love the way that the Body of Christ works. It is marvellous in itself.

the invisible sentence

One night I woke up very cold and shaking. I felt that I was in a car accident and I had been seriously injured. I knew immediately I was to start praying. I eventually forgot about the prayer until the day my friend Margaret came to visit me in Christchurch from her home in Whangaparaoa. I had picked her up the airport and when she got into my car, she appeared extremely nervous and kept pressing an invisible foot brake on the passenger side. I asked her what was going on and she relayed to me the vision of the accident I had seen weeks earlier. She had nearly crashed herself. Margaret was the person who had stepped up to pray for the person at the accident. I told her that I was also praying for the person and she said, "That's amazing," at that same moment, Lawrence (her husband) was praying for her. Now that is the Body of Christ in action.

So, what about the roles of parents? How significant it is for parents to be alert and be spiritual watchmen on the walls for their children? Parents need to understand when something is happening in the lives of their children that has a long-term effect, things that could have been cancelled if they had only been warned. Do not take lightly being a parent in the lives of your children or grandchildren. They will be bombarded on every side, especially a Christian young person. As a parent you often think you need eyes in the back of your head to watch over your children, but I am saying you need to have spiritual eyes and ears as a watchman to detect when the enemy is coming against one of your children.

So, what about the roles of parents? How significant it is for parents to be alert and be spiritual watchmen on the walls for their children?

My grandson, Luke, who lives in Australia was in danger. God alerted me. I immediately prayed for his protection and safety. Later, I phoned my daughter and said, "What was up with Luke today?"

the adventures of intercession

She said, "I thought you would be praying, Luke jumped into a covered swimming pool and got sucked in and suffocated by the cover. He was panicking and couldn't get out. He started to drown and thought it was all over."

"Something got under me and propelled me out of it," he said.

As a watchman on the wall, it is important to be able to let go of any personal involvement in the person or matter you are praying for so that God can intervene. God once said to me, "Is this your problem or mine? If it is Mine, then let it be Mine." So, it is important to remember that your children and grandchildren are not your own. They belong to God.

I had a dream about my granddaughter Jessica, and in the dream she and her friend were kidnapped. In the dream I had a visitation from her friend saying that Jessica had got away, which meant that her friend hadn't. I phoned my daughter and described the friend in the dream. The friend matched the description perfectly.

As a watchman on the wall, it is important to be able to let go of any personal involvement in the person or matter you are praying for so that God can intervene. God once said to me, "Is this your problem or mine? If it is Mine, then let it be Mine."

My daughter went to the friend's mother and in faith, told her about what I had seen. The friend's mother said that a van had been hanging around for a few days and she was quite concerned because her husband was out of town and she was living alone in their house. Jessica was going to have a sleep over. It was decided that she would not stay the night and that the two of them would be constantly watched over for the next while. As a watchman on the wall, I was able to bring a word of warning and two mothers were able to protect their children.

the invisible sentence

The Bible simply says that God places watchmen on the walls of His people. Will you let God assign *you*? Will you open *your* heart to God to be a spiritual watchman to hear and see what others may not?

The most amazing thing of all is that as a watchman on the wall you are never alone. Holy Spirit is there to guide, protect and direct you. All He requires is for you to see, hear, pray and report. The life and destiny of God's people may well rest in your faithfulness as a watchman on the wall.

seventeen

ask for a million dollars

Jesus looked straight at them and answered, "This is impossible for human beings, but for God everything is possible.

Matthew 19:26

My days were kept busy with the children and I would find that going to the toilet was often my only peace during a busy day. I could spend time there, with God, no interruptions.

One day while I was in the toilet, God spoke and said, "Ask for a million dollars." I thought, *'This is a strange request. This can't be God'*, and I ignored it. He then said again, "Ask for a million dollars."

I pondered on this and thought, *'I must have a problem with money if I can't ask for million dollars.'*

I was on a Social Welfare benefit and a million dollars would be an impossibility, but maybe God has some purpose here. So, I trusted God with this unusual request and asked for a million dollars.

One year followed another and there was still no million dollars. I had told quite a few people that I was expecting a million dollars to come to

> **One day while I was in the toilet, God spoke and said, "Ask for a million dollars."**

me, but I guess they thought I had been hearing things or that it was wishful thinking.

Paul got out of prison and still the million dollars hadn't arrived. Then, 13 years after that word, Pillars, the organisation I founded, won a $1.3 million dollar contract from the Department of Corrections to pilot a prisoner and family pre-and post-reintegration programme. I knew that this had to be the million dollars.

After God had answered my request, one person I had told that the million dollars was on the way said, "Well it wasn't a million dollars it was $1.3 million."

To this Paul said, "The extra $300,000 was the interest because my wife had to wait so long."

eighteen

the beginnings of Pillars

Go and gather the leaders of Israel together and tell them that I, the Lord, the God of their ancestors, the God of Abraham, Isaac, and Jacob, appeared to you. Tell them that I have come to them and have seen what the Egyptians are doing to them. I have decided that I will bring them out of Egypt (bondage), where they are being treated cruelly, and will take them to a rich and fertile land (the promised land – a land full of milk and honey) — the land of the Canaanites, the Hittites, the Amorites, the Perizzites, the Hivites, and the Jebusites.

Exodus 3:16-17

On 19 May 1988, Kate turned five and started school. I got down on my knees and asked God what he wanted me to do with my spare time now. God spoke to me and said, "Read Exodus 3 and 4." It was about Moses bringing the Israelites out of Egypt. These words jumped off the page, *"Bring my people out of bondage and lead them into the promised land, a land full of milk and honey."*

I knew this was the calling to start the support for families and children of prisoners. I had no idea where to start so I asked God to put people on my path to help.

That day I heard an advert on the radio about the Christian Family Movement that ran support groups for single parents. So, I thought, this sounds like an interesting group. Maybe I should start there? That night Paul phoned me from the prison and said he had just read an article in the paper about the Christian Family Movement. He knew I was keen to investigate support groups, "Maybe you should start there?" So, I took this as the go ahead.

That night, God gave me the mandate to start the support group by giving me the scripture Isaiah 60, *Arise, Jerusalem, and shine like the sun; The glory of the Lord is shining on you! Other nations will be covered by darkness, But on you the light of the Lord will shine; The brightness of his presence will be with you. Nations will be drawn to your light, And kings to the dawning of your new day* —Isaiah 60:1-3.

I felt I was on a real mission. Whereas, as a child, I had a deep desire to be a missionary, I was now given that calling to start. But not overseas. It was here in New Zealand.

> **God gave me the name 'Pillars'... "I see the men and women supporting their loved-ones in prison as 'My Pillars'. They are raising their children and visiting their loved-ones in prison under extreme adverse circumstances."**

God made it clear that it was not to be a Christian organisation—that it was for everyone.

For six months, the Christian Family Movement trained Debra, Reg (my father-in-law), and me to facilitate support groups and they provided us with professional supervision. During that time, before the group started, God gave me the name 'Pillars'. I asked Him what that meant?

He said, "Where the public sees politicians, celebrities and renowned public people as the Pillars of Society, I see the men and women supporting their loved-ones in prison as 'My Pillars'. They are raising their children and visiting their loved-ones in prison under extreme adverse circumstances. They are ostracized by their communities and unsupported by the prison system. Their good works go unnoticed, but not by Me. Also, Pillars standing together give strength to one another, but a Pillar standing alone will weather without support around it and collapse under the stresses and strains of life."

What started as a potluck tea at 5.30pm finished at 3.00am; ten hours of sharing experiences with one another, crying with one another and supporting one another.

The interesting thing was that as I didn't speak to other families when I visited the prison, as everyone kept to themselves, how would I ever make contact with these women? Every prison was different, and there appeared to be a prison culture at Paparua Prison where families didn't appear to mix and mingle. This, of course, would ensure that the men could keep control of their wives from behind prison walls. So, everyone just stood in line and waited their turn to go into visits and no one spoke to each other. So, finding people to come to a support group was a challenge. But God made a way.

I met 12 women all who had a loved-one in prison. I met them in the streets, at church, and at Social Welfare all in the week before we started. And met them all outside of the prison environment. The first meeting began with 12 women with children all who had a partner in prison. What started as a potluck tea at 5.30pm finished at 3.00am; ten hours of sharing experiences with one another, crying with one another and supporting one another. We realised that we had been trying to cope alone all this time and we needed support. At last, we all had a safe place to talk about our situations and help one another. It felt great.

Up until then there had been no support for prisoners' families. There was no support for us. You could get food parcels, handouts, etc. but no hands-up support. You almost needed a degree in communication to visit someone in prison. Sitting opposite them for two and a half hours was so artificial. Maintaining our family relationships behind prison walls was not easy and, on top of that, we were mostly ostracised by the community and had little, if no, support.

Paul had met an adult educator, Bryan Gray in the prison and he introduced him to me. Bryan and later Jennifer Leahy facilitated the day and evening support groups and provided us with coping skills and workshops on maintaining our relationships apart and coping alone.

At the support group we talked about what we now call the 'invisible sentence', the sentence that is served outside of the wire by the families left behind. We talked about the effects on our children from the trauma at arrest through to being called a 'jail bird' in the school yard.

We worried about our children going down the wrong path and ending up in prison themselves and we did not want that for them.

We very quickly started to get a clear picture of what was needed for families like ours. We would develop a framework of support and we would find the funding to do it. We would advocate for the rights of children to have safe and meaningful contact with their parent in prison and be properly supported and cared for in their parent's absence. We would reduce the harm caused by stigma of our situation that our children had absolutely no say in. This was how the charity Pillars was born.

In the beginning we were not taken seriously by the Department of Justice and Social Welfare. In fact, we were tainted by the community who looked upon us with distrust. We then found that when we dressed

the beginnings of Pillars

up in suits and took a briefcase with us that the meetings went a little better. There was never anything in the briefcase, we just kept it in the office as a prop for important meetings.

There was a meeting early in Pillars history where the women presented their ideas to one prison boss. We all felt the meeting went well, but after we left we could hear him and another officer both laughing about us behind the closed door. It was even said that we set up Pillars to get our husbands out of prison early.

God reminded me of the scripture, 1 Timothy 2: 1-3, *First of all, then, I urge that petitions, prayers, requests, and thanksgivings be offered to God for all people; for kings and all others who are in authority, that we may live a quiet and peaceful life with all reverence toward God and with proper conduct. This is good and it pleases God our Saviour.*

So I decided to put him on my prayer hit list.

Several years later, I was approached by that same boss who said to me, "I have been watching Pillars and I think you are a Kiwi battler. You are really starting to achieve change." He then gave us a space at the back of the Addington Prison for an office and youth centre at a peppercorn rental of $5 a year.

Once it had got out around the prison grapevine about the group in Christchurch, family members would contact me to start a Pillars group in their area. Debra and I had attended a Community Education conference and educators from regions around New Zealand gave their facilitation support if we started up a Pillars in their area. By the end of the second year there were seven

> **We all felt the meeting went well, but after we left we could hear him and another officer all laughing about us behind the closed door. It was even said that we set up Pillars to get our husbands out of prison early.**

support groups up and running around New Zealand all starting through the vision of a person who had a family member in prison backed by a community educator.

My pastor at the time became our unofficial Pillars pastor and he would pop in to say "Hi" when the support group was meeting in Christchurch. He never put any religious pressure on anyone and never judged anyone but was always available when required.

One day he arrived and, as usual, a support group was taking place. One of the ladies had been diagnosed with a cancerous lump in her breast and she was really worried about it. She asked Pastor Geoff if he would pray for her.

So, in the room filled with cigarette smoke, swearing and concern, he prayed, and the lump instantly disappeared. The women were amazed and couldn't believe God would do such a thing. They had heard me harking on about God for some time and now they had seen a miracle for themselves. The women all got very chatty and wanted to know more about God. We talked about food provision so we decided that we would all ask God right there and then, to provide for our food for the next week.

At the meeting the following week, the women excitedly reported back about instances when food had arrived unexpectedly and just when needed.

> **At the meeting the following week, the women excitedly reported back about instances when food had arrived unexpectedly and just when needed.**

nineteen

Paul is released from prison

The next morning the Roman authorities sent police officers with the order, "Let those men go." So the jailer told Paul, "The officials have sent an order for you and Silas to be released. You may leave, then, and go in peace."

Acts 16:35-36

The scripture is about Paul in the Bible, but it definitely relates to my Paul when his time was up.

The 11th of April is a significant day. It was the day Paul was sentenced to 11 years in prison, and our 13th wedding anniversary. On 11th April, seven years later, it was our 20th wedding anniversary the day he was released.

It was March. Paul was meeting with the Parole Board for the second time. There was no expectation that he would be released.

At the first Parole Board meeting, Paul was told he had applied six months earlier than he was entitled to. However, he was granted home leave. Nevertheless, in the six months after that meeting, he only got one day leave and one overnight leave.

The first home leave was amazing, having him sitting in the car with me leaving the prison. I had to pinch myself to see if it was real.

Paul said he would come home as a visitor. As far as he was concerned, I was running the family and had been for the last seven years. When he came home the first time, he was met at the door by our rescue cat. Honey didn't like anybody. She had been abused as a kitten and never got over it. She would grab your ankles and bite hard as you walked past but she just bowled up to Paul and jumped up to him. She knew he was one of the family.

It was terrible when the home leave was over and we had to take him back to the prison. It was painful and we all hated that.

For the second Parole Board meeting, I decided to write and ask to meet with them. I had not heard whether other families had met with the Parole Board previously, but I felt it was important since he would be coming home to live with us. They needed to meet with Paul's family face to face. I was elated when I received a letter saying I could attend.

There were no computers in those days, so I wrote a letter in my own handwriting and had it photocopied to give each Board member on the day. In the letter I asked if they would please release him on the 11th April for our 20th wedding anniversary.

Much to my astonishment, they agreed. They believed he wasn't a risk to the community and would be better off at home with his family.

When he officially received his final release date, I only had two weeks to prepare. We didn't tell the children because I knew they wouldn't go to

Paul is released from prison

school and we wanted some time together that day.

I picked him up and brought him home. We then went into the city to pick up his Steps to Freedom release money as he had no clothes. I had kept the clothes he had before he went away but they were now seven years old. I picked up a pair of undies and 'poof' the elastic disintegrated, and the clothes looked like something out of the hippy era anyway. So, we decided we would get some clothes at a second-hand shop.

On the way into the city we met a guy who had recently been released. His wife worked at a clothing store. She came from a Christian family and they decided they would deck Paul out with new clothes. It was a lovely feeling going home that day knowing he had normal clothes and new ones at that.

A requirement of his release was that Paul had to report to the Probation Service within 48 hours. This was a mission. It took three days to get there. We would walk out the door, get halfway and would have to turn back. Paul was not used to the city and its busyness. Rolleston Prison was a quiet place like an old people's home, and we had come from Oamaru, a small town. Paul could not cope with the traffic, the traffic lights and even opening a bank account was a mission. He didn't know how to get money from the money machines or how to fill up the car at a petrol station. The world had changed so much in seven years.

The children were overjoyed that Dad was home, but it was quite traumatic for Kate who had never had him living with us.

The children were overjoyed that Dad was home, but it was quite traumatic for Kate who had never had him living with us. I can remember when Paul was going to be released, she asked where he would sleep and I said with me in my bed and she said, "Oh yuck."

Housing New Zealand decided to sell the house in Durham Street, so they moved us to a five-bedroomed home in Hoon Hay. While there, we were notified that all Housing New Zealand houses would be put up to market rental rates in 12 months. We decided we would use the 12 months to save for a deposit on a house. Paul had got a job building and I went from voluntary into paid work at Pillars. We saved like crazy and had enough to put down a deposit on our own four-bedroom home. It was a relief getting back into the housing market.

We were living in our own home when Paul decided to go building out on his own.

We had our house and contents insured with an insurance company and I had always dutifully paid the premiums on time. We had gone around garage sales and procured several hand tools and Paul had invested in some electric drills and saws and needed them insured. We went to the insurance company to fill in the various forms. One of the forms asked about criminal records. Paul asked the agent, "Does this mean if I have been in prison?" to which he answered, "Yes." So, we ticked the 'yes' box.

The agent went and spoke to a supervisor and came back and said, "We don't want you as our customer as you have a criminal record."

The agent went and spoke to a supervisor and came back and said, "We don't want you as our customer as you have a criminal record."

We said, "But the prison sentence has been served," to which he said, "We can't guarantee your character. So, we don't want to insure you."

I then said, "But my house and contents are here and they've been insured here for years," to which he said, "We will be cancelling these policies too."

I was astounded. There was a mortgage on the house and the requirement was that it be insured. Now what was I to do?

I had just paid a further premium a couple of days before and, hey presto, the cheque I had sent arrived back in the post. It was a hard two weeks knowing that our house was not insured.

Paul is released from prison

As it turned out, Paul had met an old school friend who had visited the prison with his church. He was an insurance broker. We decided to contact him. We had to prepare CV's and a background of our situation so he could lobby insurance companies to take us on. We were delighted when we were accepted by one company.

the invisible sentence

twenty

the earthquake angels

*Remember to welcome strangers into your homes.
There were some who did that and welcomed angels
without knowing it.*

Hebrews 13:2

In the early hours of 4 September 2010, Christchurch and the surrounding areas experienced a major 7.1 magnitude earthquake. We were in bed asleep when the earthquake hit. Initially, we thought a plane had crashed because we could hear the engines roaring but could smell no fuel, so we discounted that. Paul had built our house to be pretty much earthquake proof and we knew that most other houses were not, so we thought we may be the only survivors. We spontaneously dressed in the dark. I could only find one shoe so went outside with just one shoe on stepping over glass and furniture as we went.

Once outside, we were surprised that the houses around us were still standing. The neighbours had all congregated outside of their gates in their pyjamas in the hope that there was a sign that someone else was alive. It was a relief and an amazement that no one was hurt. Someone then got a phone call and we heard that buildings had come down in the central city, but no injuries were reported. We eventually all headed back to our own homes.

We were so traumatised that we didn't go back into the house but sat outside in Paul's truck for the rest of the night and listened to the radio.

At dawn, we cleaned up the house, which was littered with broken dishes and furniture. Food had spewed out from the pantry and dishes out of the cupboards. Paul started to sweep up outside and found that our goldfish had been catapulted from the pond.

> **Food had spewed out from the pantry and dishes out of the cupboards. Paul started to sweep up outside and found that our goldfish had been catapulted from the pond.**

I investigated the garage and found that my car was munted. We had tins of paint left over from the house on shelves and they had opened up and spilled themselves over my car. My car was one of many damaged in the earthquake and 'munted' became a Christchurch household word for almost anything damaged.

After this quake came a series of thousands of other quakes closely following. We learned to live with earthquakes and Christchurch became known as Quake City.

Several of the Pillars families had lost their homes and we, as workers, went into survival mode ensuring they were safely housed, had access to food and water and were connected to their immediate community. We developed a new way of working.

Then at 12.51pm on Tuesday 22 February 2011, a deadly earthquake struck. Compared to the 7.1 quake in September, it had a magnitude of 6.3 but was closer to the surface causing severe damage in Christchurch and Lyttelton, killing 185 people and injuring several thousand.

At the time, all our social workers and mentoring coordinators were out visiting families and mentors. Megan, our administrator, and I were

the earthquake angels

the only staff at the Pillars Centre. The shaking was so strong we could not stand up. I immediately phoned Paul as I thought I would get in before the phones stopped working through the lack of electricity because of earthquake damage to let him know I was okay. He was at the pizza parlour we owned in Hills Road.

From where I was, I was concerned that the slab concrete walls that were secured by bolts would break and we would both be crushed. They were rattling so loudly you couldn't hear yourself think. I yelled at Megan to get out, but both she and I could not move. Megan was under a desk and I was crawling on the floor trying to open the front door. Ten seconds later, the earthquake subsided enough so we could get outside into the car park where we held onto the backs of our cars for support. Then suddenly, the place started flooding. I first thought it was a broken pipe but later discovered it was called 'liquefaction'. I had never seen this before and in seconds it was up to my knees and flowing like a river.

I said to Megan, "We must go back in and get what we need." That was scary as we were both traumatised from the event. I told Megan to throw the server up on the desk. I was concerned we would lose our electronic documents due to the flooding.

From where I was, I was concerned that the slab concrete walls that were secured by bolts would break and we would both be crushed. They were rattling so loudly you couldn't hear yourself think.

Our IT support said later it was the best thing we ever did. I did a mental check of my office to see what had to be removed. I threw important documents up onto my desk, grabbed my laptop, handbag and car keys and left the building. Megan and I decided it wasn't safe where we were and got into our cars and drove down flooded streets to an area that was safe. We waited for staff to turn up, but I hoped they would just go home.

the invisible sentence

By now, the streets were full of vehicles, with people evacuating the city and trying to get home. I ventured up Fitzgerald Avenue in my car. I could see people streaming out of the Central City on foot. Many had injuries and were covered in blood. It was like a war zone. People were supporting each other; the scene was chaotic. There were aftershocks that kept rumbling through on average every five minutes. I slowly drove along the flooded avenue in the hope that liquefaction wouldn't come into my car. I was pleased there were cars in front of me because I was selfishly thinking if the ground opened up, they would go in first. I had the radio on listening to the voice of Willie Jackson on Radio Live. It was soothing to me and I held onto that voice with all I had.

I ventured up Fitzgerald Avenue in my car. I could see people streaming out of the Central City on foot. Many had injuries and were covered in blood. It was like a war zone.

I had no idea what had happened in the central city but I knew it must be bad. I could see billowing clouds of dust and debris enveloping the city like a mushroom. I knew Paul was safe but I hoped that my children out in outlying Rangiora were okay.

Thirty minutes later I had hardly moved up the avenue. I was frantic to get home, but the place was gridlocked. Then a stranger came over to my car. He was very well dressed, like something you would see in the 1940s. He stood right out as strange. He had donned a white satin scarf and wore a cap. I had only seen my grandfather wear one of those when I was little. He knocked at my window, I wound it down and he said, "You need to know that the bridge is down up ahead. You're not going to get through," to which I said, "Thanks mate." I then expected him to go to the car behind me. I looked behind and the man had disappeared. He didn't approach any other vehicles and he was nowhere to be seen. He had just vanished into thin air.

I then had to decide how I would get home. Should I abandon my vehicle and just walk? Then as I drove slowly toward Armagh Street, I heard the Lord say, "Turn here." It was like he had his arms open inviting me to turn. But it was back toward the city where people were fleeing from.

But joy overcame my spirit as I turned and went back into the city. I was the only car on the road. People flooding out from the city were looking at me strangely as I drove past. But it all seemed so right. I got to the intersection at Madras Street and was confronted with what I call a "big swirl of porridge" (liquefaction) and there was a man (or an angel) giving me directions to go around it and onto the one-way system. As I drove around it, I hoped I wouldn't fall in.

So, I turned north and headed up Madras Street, crossed over the Kilmore Street bridge, which I now call 'Freedom Bridge'. I was the only car on that road. Once over the river I was on my way home. It took me five minutes to get into my driveway. It was reported later that for some people in Fitzgerald Avenue it took several hours to get home on that fateful day.

the invisible sentence

twenty-one

tea with the governor general

*Then the angel said to me,
"Write this, 'Happy are those who have been invited
to the wedding feast of the Lamb." And the angel
added, "These are the true words of God."*

Revelation 19:9

In 2012, I was acknowledged in the New Year Honours list by being appointed a Member of the New Zealand Order of Merit for my services to the community. Some months before, I had received a very official looking letter in the post. The envelope had a rich textured feel and I had never received a letter quite like it before. I was cautious opening it as I didn't want to rip the envelope as I am a lover of nice stationery. I wondered what could possibly be so serious that I would get a letter like this. Once opened, I gingerly removed the letter and read it, and I was dumbfounded at what jumped out at me on the page. At the time, Paul and I were sitting in our car about to head off to the supermarket. Paul said, "Who is the letter from," and I could not get anything to come out of my mouth. I don't believe in awards for people, I believe you do good where you can on the earth as part of your rent here. But then, I found out that my Pillars family had put me up for the award so I felt it was representing them the families, children and mentors who are the Pillars. I felt I would be letting them down if I declined the invitation.

So, in May that year, I was summoned to Government House to an investiture and was presented with the MNZM by the then, Governor General Sir Jerry Mateparae.

It was a right royal affair and I felt immensely proud in accepting the award on behalf of the children and families of prisoners in New Zealand. I was saddened that my parents couldn't be there to enjoy the celebrations as they had both died but they would have been immensely proud.

I was summoned to Government House to an investiture and was presented with the MNZM by the then, Governor General Sir Jerry Mateparae.

The investiture ceremony was very official, but it was the meal afterwards...

Everyone who had received an award on that day was invited to tea with the Governor General and Lady Janine. We all sat around a huge, exquisitely carved table. It was so highly polished you could see your face in it. We all had our own seats delicately embroidered with a name of a location in New Zealand. I sat in the Rotorua seat. Sir Jerry and Lady Janine sat at the side and in the middle. Sir Jerry announced, "At our dinner table we don't sit together as couples, we sit with other people we don't know," so we were separated from our partners. Paul sat at the head of the table and I sat at the other end.

Then Sir Jerry introduced us all and when he came to Paul he said, "And this is Paul McFelin, and he is why Pillars started." I would say people are still trying to work that one out. What made it so funny was that Paul was sitting next to the police commissioner's wife.

I was sitting beside a guy who worked in some high-level intelligence environment and I asked him, "How many people work at your place," and he said, "More than one." Much to my amusement, he couldn't even tell me how many people were employed where he worked.

The meal was a culinary delight; something you would only experience once in your lifetime. It had four courses and it was something you would pay big dollars for at a top restaurant. Each plate had the insignia of the Crown etched in gold. It was as if we were eating at Buckingham Palace.

There was raw fish for the entree, then a sorbet, which was just exquisite, then lamb cooked in a fine pastry and we finished off with a baked white pear that was just shimmering and glistening on the plate. It was adorned with a beautiful cake with cream cheese and hokey pokey ice cream on the side. There was also a liquid in an exceedingly small glass that came with the dessert. None of us knew what to do with that.

We all had matching cutlery, dishes and glasses formally set before us. Behind us, we each had our own waiter dressed in a neat, grey crisp uniform wearing white gloves. As they moved there was not a sound. In unison, they would place our course in front of us then quickly step back. My friend from intelligence ended up calling them the 'swimmers'. Looking from the head of the table where Paul was sitting it looked like a rowing eight putting their boats in the water.

Then there were the glasses. My mother had taught me table etiquette, to always start at the outside of your cutlery and move into the middle for each course, but she never taught me about the glasses. I had five glasses in front of me and each course used a different glass for a different drink. I did not have a clue what they were for and nor did any of the other guests. So, we all kept an eye on the Governor General to see what glass he was drinking from. We had all sorts of different drinks, and I drunk well over my usual half a glass of alcohol quota.

> **Each plate had the insignia of the Crown etched in gold. It was as if we were eating at Buckingham Palace.**

the invisible sentence

But the funniest thing of the day was the fluid that came out with the dessert. We didn't know what to do with that; whether you drank it or poured it over the dessert. By this time, we had all had a few drinks too many and we were getting merry and were all laughing and giggling away. So we watched the Governor General and he picked up the little glass of liquid and drank it and we all burst out laughing. We thought it might have been the sauce to go on the pudding.

Throughout the meal I had a deep sense of God showing me what the marriage supper of the Lamb will be with Him. If I thought this was amazing how much more amazing will that be.

After tea, we moved to the main lounge and had coffee and liqueurs then three hours after it all had started, a gong went and the Governor General and Lady Janine left immediately. It was a big thrill and a privilege to meet so many people who had made such huge contributions to our country. A group of us were invited back to attend an informal lunch the next day. What an unbelievable experience.

twenty-two

the end of the beginning

*I will give you back what you lost in the years when swarms of locusts ate your crops. It was I who sent this army against you. Now you will have plenty to eat, and be satisfied. You will praise the LORD your God, who has done wonderful things for you.
My people will never be despised again. Then, Israel, you will know that I am among you and that I, the Lord, am your God and there is no other.
My people will never be despised again.*

Joel 2:25-27

As time went on, our children grew up and three of them moved to Australia. Our son met a young woman, Caroline, and they became engaged. They started talking marriage. Her stepfather was high up in the Queensland police. We were concerned how Paul could get to the wedding because with a prison record he would need a visa. The father-in-law said to just jump on a plane and be open about your situation when you arrive. He said he would sort it at the border.

We booked our tickets and the day of the wedding loomed. Kate, Glen her husband, Paul and I boarded the plane set for Australia. We were all seated when an immigration officer boarded the plan and approached Paul and asked for a chat. It turned out that he wouldn't be travelling that day as times and proceedings had changed and vetting was done prior to departure. He had already been refused entry even before we left. He would not be allowed to attend his own son's wedding. The plane was held up for 30 minutes while they searched the hull for his luggage. Once found, he left. My daughter was devastated and cried all the way to Australia.

When we arrived, it was discovered Paul had been given Kate's luggage, and she ended up with Paul's. All her wedding gear was back in Christchurch and the only clothes she had were what she was standing in.

I decided after this experience I would put up a case to the Australian Immigration Department so Paul could visit his children in Australia. He was no risk to the community. I wrote a strong case for Paul, arguing each clause of the Immigration Act and, in particular, that about 'illegal aliens'.

Paul had been talking with the department and it looked promising that the application would be successful. We had planned a trip for my daughter's 40th birthday and we notified the department about it. I purchased my ticket and decided to purchase one for Paul once his approval had come through. One week before we were to leave, we still hadn't heard. I checked the plane tickets and there were no seats available to the Gold Coast or Brisbane. We were devastated. The evening before I was to leave, the approval to travel came through. It was bittersweet because he couldn't travel as all flights were full. But I thought, I'll just have another last-minute look to see if there is at least one seat available—and lo-and-behold there was one seat available on my flight. We booked it immediately and didn't even get to tell the children that Paul was coming.

He had already been refused entry even before we left. He would not be allowed to attend his own son's wedding.

I can remember when we first arrived at the airport an immigration officer called out, "All the bad boys please line up here?" Everyone laughed. So off Paul went along with several other men all dressed in Hawaiian shirts and shorts looking like over 60s tourists. They looked like ordinary old men, not ex-prisoners.

Once we got through customs and out of the airport the children arrived to pick us up. I can still remember their faces when they saw Paul. Lisa said the F-word. She normally doesn't swear. She later said she thought she had seen a ghost.

Paul is a really gifted builder. We split our section, sold our house on the front and built an architecturally designed house on the back section. We were fortunate that during the 12 months it took to build the house that we could rent a property right next door. Once it was finished, we moved into the new house and lived happily there for several years.

> **Lisa said the F-word. She normally doesn't swear. She later said she thought she had seen a ghost.**

Prior to the 2010 earthquakes we had discussed selling the house and moving into the Cashmere hills. We always wanted a hill section for the view but properties in Cashmere were well out of our price range.

So, we prayed and asked God to provide us with a section. After the prayer, several people in their general conversation with me would say, 'the hills are alive', for no apparent reason. I knew God was trying to tell me something but I had no idea what it was.

At this time, Paul was back running a pizza parlour and we decided to put our house and pizza business on the market. We sold both all in the same week, just after the earthquakes.

As it turned out, people were coming off the hills in droves as the earthquakes had caused huge devastation there and people had lost their homes and were fearful. Many said they would never return. The prices of sections on the hill dropped dramatically and then I understood what the word, 'the hills are alive,' meant. It referred to the earthquakes.

the invisible sentence

On April 11, 2020, we celebrated three anniversaries. The anniversary of Paul's sentence, the anniversary of his release and our 50th wedding anniversary.

That meant that there was an opportunity for us to purchase a site.

We saw an advert for a section in the Christchurch Press newspaper and went to look at it. It was a 1012 square metres (a quarter acre) with a panoramic view. It was amazing and was perfect. We had to submit a closed bid, so we didn't know what interest others had in it. We prayed separately and both came up with the exact same price, which was less than half of what it was worth. We weren't the highest price by any means, but the others had purchase conditions due to the risk and work involved. The site was once described as the 'Rolls Royce' of hill sites by the developers who'd built their own house on it. We bought it off an ex-North Otago couple. Small world!

Paul built a one-bedroom apartment at the back of the property where we are currently living while he is building the big house in front. So much for retirement.

Our children have all left home, but we want the house to be used by our family when they visit, travelling ministers and people needing suitable temporary accommodation. We have an apartment attached to give us extra income to supplement our pension.

On 11th April 2020, we celebrated three anniversaries. The anniversary of Paul's sentence, the anniversary of his release and our 50th wedding anniversary. There was no big party or celebration. We did though get a card from the Prime Minister, the Governor General of New Zealand, the Mayor of Christchurch and other well-wishers. It was during the Covid-19 lockdown, so I baked and iced a cake, cut up some old beads and pressed them into the icing making a big 50 on the cake. We then unceremoniously cut it together and sat down and ate it in front of the television all on our own.

my lessons and learnings

Listen and acknowledge a child when they talk about the spiritual realm

It is important that when a child discloses that they have seen demons or angels that you believe them. Tell them that God and the angels are stronger than the demons and that they cannot hurt them because they are in God's bubble. That they can tell the demons to go in Jesus' name and they must go. Ensure that they feel safe at night and can come to you at any time day or night when they are scared.

Hate judgmental religion with a holy hatred

Have a holy hatred of judgmental religion with its rules and regulations its systems and traditions, its acceptance of some and not of others. I am talking about the institutions here, not the people in them. Unfortunately, the world judges Christians as being 'judgmentally religious' and sadly those of us who seek not to be like that are tarnished with this same brush. This is the one thing that has saddened me through most on my journey with God. The world needs to know that Christianity is a relationship with Almighty God who intimately knows each one of us and wants the best for all.

God is pure love
God is love and He created the world and its people because He is love. Without Him, there would be no love in the world. Therefore, we should love, respect and be kind to each other. We are called to love not to judge. God accepts you just the way you are and loves you just the way you are whether you are Christian or not.

Forgiveness is God's good news
All humans are simultaneously sinful and loved. Everyone, no matter how much wrong they have done can know that they have been totally forgiven by God and empowered by Him to live free from the guilt and shame that keeps them locked into harmful habits. When we yield our hearts and minds to Christ and His forgiveness, we will live the new life that God has designed us for in a loving relationship with Him. This is truly good news for everyone.

Care for children
Always take time to listen and hear what children are saying. Always tell them the truth according to their age. The most psychologically damaging thing you can stay to a child is a lie that they find out later was not true. Help them believe in themselves and support them to face challenges with confidence. Tell them that mistakes are opportunities to grow and that they can achieve anything if they are persistent no matter what their circumstances. Ensure that they have a positive life.

Witnessing is walking in God's power
God will always orchestrate the witness, not you. It must be in partnership with the Holy Spirit and have inexplicable power behind it. Tell people about the love of Jesus so they can reach out to God and personally experience it.

Develop an awareness of His presence
Christ lives in us and never leaves us. As we develop an awareness of his abiding presence in and around us it fills us with assurance of his faithfulness and great love.

Walk intimately with God
Walking intimately with Him is a freedom not a religious duty. It is a relationship built on trust for each other. It's a covenant relationship between God and His people, mediated by Jesus, that He brings us into. When you pray, it's either God's problem or your problem. Best make it God's problem. Take big risks with God, he will always come through. God does the impossible. We have the Holy Spirit on earth who is our Helper, Comforter and Giver of Graces.

The promises in the Bible are yes and amen
Get a deep grounding of the promises in the Bible. Speaking these out is essential for Him to release tremendous power through you. The Bible is not just a book, the scriptures in it bring forth power. Learning and speaking out the promises of God over our circumstances are keys to possessing them and turning around a situation. Don't doubt God.

Pray without ceasing
God calls watchmen to give a warning message in order to "rescue men and women from impending destruction." Practice keeping your Spirit quiet and keep it alert day and night so you can hear God speak then act on His voice. We must remain vigilant. It is a partnership between you and God. When you know God is speaking, you must act immediately.

Steward His power

We must properly steward His power. God has placed us in Christ. When we ground ourselves in this truth our lives will change and our character will reflect the God in whom we dwell. But you don't have to wait to be a mature Christian to allow God to use you. You can begin to operate in the Spirit the moment Christ enters your heart.

This was true in my life. I experienced and continue to experience many encounters and many moments of God's power and these have shaped who I am today. We should never see ourselves as not being equipped with God's power. We are people of power because we belong to Jesus Christ who has all power and authority. He has given us the power to overcome the enemy and nothing can harm us.

The question is, do we really believe we have such power as children of God? If you don't, you need to change your mind-set. God is not a liar. God's name is hallowed. His name is power, so you are all powerful in His name.

God should be at the centre of everything

Most of our relationship with God is confined to asking Him to bless us. We ask God for healing, for success, for financial security. We ask Him to bless our family, to bless our jobs, to bless our plans.

It may be shameful for some of us to realise that more often than not, we are at the centre of our prayers rather than Christ. The result of this is the subtle belief that Christ exists for our benefit. This distortion breaks God's heart and leads us far away from truly knowing Him for who He really is, our King and Creator!

glossary

Addington Remand Prison: A place of confinement for inmates awaiting their sentence.

Cell: A small room where a prisoner is housed within a prison.

Court Hearing: An official meeting held at a Court.

Damascus Road experience: A dramatic sudden conversion experience.

Farmlet: A small lifestyle block of land.

Glory: The manifestation of God's presence as perceived by humans.

Incarcerated: Another word for imprisonment.

Inmate: Person in prison.

Intercession: The action of saying a prayer on behalf of another as led by the Holy Spirit.

Invisible sentence: The sentence served outside the prison wire by the families who have someone in prison.

Jail: A place for the confinement of people accused or convicted of a crime.

Kaumatua: a Māori elder.

Lag: Another word for a long sentence.

Liquefaction: Conversion of soil into a fluid-like mass during an earthquake or other seismic event.

the *invisible* sentence

Lockdown: The confining of prisoners to their cells, typically in order to regain control during a riot.

Lolly: An edible sweet.

Mahi: Work or an activity. Mana. Dictionaries usually translate this as 'authority, prestige, pride, or status'. Fluent speakers of Māori are aware that this concept in Māori can mean something else that is not always expressed well by the English translations.

Māori: The indigenous people of New Zealand.

Mongrel Mob: The Mongrel Mob (sometimes self-labelled as the Mighty Mongrel Mob) is an organised street gang based in New Zealand that has a network of more than thirty chapters throughout the country.

Paparua medium-security prison: A place of confinement for people serving their sentence who have been classified as 'medium security'.

Paremoremo Maximum Security Prison: A place of confinement for people serving their sentence who have been classified as 'maximum security'.

Parole Board: A panel of people who decide whether an offender should be released from prison on parole after serving at least a minimum portion of their sentence as prescribed by the sentencing judge.

Pipi: An edible shellfish found in the sand at low tide.

Prison: Another word for jail.

Probation Service: A place where offenders and prisoners report to as part of following standard and, maybe, special conditions after release when they are in the community. If an offender doesn't follow the conditions set, they could be fined, get another sentence or be sent back to prison.

glossary

Propped: When prisoners refused to co-operate or do any work for a purpose—a strike.

Rolleston Minimum Security Prison: A place of confinement for people serving their sentence who have been classified as 'minimum security'.

Trial: A formal examination of evidence by a judge, typically before a jury, in order to decide guilt in a case of criminal or civil proceedings.

Sally port: A holding area between two doors or barricades so that prisoners can be moved to another area.

Screw: The slang name for prison officer, prison warden or guard.

Sentence: The punishment decided for (an offender).

Seraphim: The highest-ranking angels of God (above angels, archangels, cherubim, etc.)

Speaking in tongues: Sometimes referred to as glossolalia. The phenomenon of speaking in an unknown language, especially in religious worship. It is practised especially by Pentecostal and charismatic Christians.

Steps to Freedom: Money given to prisoners on release to establish themselves in the community.

Whānau: An extended family or community of related families based on a Māori and tribal world view.

Word of Knowledge: The ability to know facts about a situation or a spiritual principle that could not have been known by natural means. This allows someone to see a situation as God sees it.

the invisible sentence

children of incarcerated parents

There are about 23,000 children in New Zealand with parents behind bars and they are nine and a half times more likely to end up in prison themselves without the right support.

New Zealand has one of the highest rates of imprisonment in the western world. When I hear statistics like that, my first thought is not the financial cost of building prisons, staffing them, and housing the prisoners, but the human costs borne by the children whose parents are behind bars right now.

The clamour for larger prison sentences is louder than ever, but in depriving criminals of their freedom, we are also depriving thousands of children of their parents. Children love their parents and, through no fault of their own, they are suddenly separated from one or both parents and left to cope alone.

They are frequently required to move from their family environment and provided with little if any specialised support or counselling. Many of these children suffer physical, mental and emotional problems that deteriorate over time, with some described by the Pillars' researcher as 'walking powder kegs' badly in need of high-quality intervention.

Chronic bed-wetting, nightmares, anxiety, anger and depression, aggravated eczema and asthma are common. They bear the punishment for the sins of their parent/s and are often treated badly by others and considered guilty by association.

Sometimes sending a parent to prison can bring changes for the better; for example, when a sexually abusive father is punished or the neglected child of an alcoholic mother finally gets enough to eat but, mostly youngsters are worse off and both caregivers and children attribute that to the absence of the imprisoned parents rather than their criminality.

> **Please get involved in your area in supporting our most vulnerable children left behind when their parent goes to prison, the children of prisoners.**

Children are often ashamed and don't know how to reconcile their love for their parent with the rejection from the community. They are often so humiliated by their situation they don't tell friends. Friends are their lifelines, and it is devastating if that support is cut off. Once that happens, they don't want to go to school truancy happens, and they drop out. This begins the spiral downhill. The cost of that spiral is staggering. Former Justice Minister, Simon Power said, "A male teenager on the wrong side of the tracks, heading towards a life of crime will cost society three million dollars over his lifetime."

As founder of Pillars, I continue to draw attention to the invisible stigma that is in our communities. Stopping these children from going to prison in the first place makes better sense than locking people up at the Government's and taxpayer's expense.

We all want positive futures for our children that doesn't involve a prison sentence. Please get involved in your area in supporting our most vulnerable children left behind when their parent goes to prison, the children of prisoners.

about Pillars

Pillars was founded by me in 1988, and today I am proud that it has developed into a national organisation upholding the rights of children of prisoners. For 32 years I worked tirelessly to lead Pillars and to advocate for the rights of these vulnerable children.

I have been told that Pillars punches above its weight in the international field of development, policies, and practices. I introduced the Children's Bill of Rights into the New Zealand Corrections system, pioneered family support programmes both in prisons and the community and was involved in setting up the International Coalition of Children of Incarcerated parents (INCCIP), with Pillars hosting their first conference in New Zealand.

I am proud to say that there is now a team of specialist staff delivering Pillars services throughout New Zealand, but I believe the real heroes of the programmes are the volunteers who give up their weekends and spare time to mentor hundreds of children who are facing some of the most challenging and difficult times in their lives.

My dream is easily realised… "Mentor these children and we could halve a nation's crime rate in 10 years."

the invisible sentence

about the author

Verna McFelin has dedicated her life to part of the criminal justice system most of us forget to remember, the families, especially the children of offenders. The work Verna has done with Pillars, an organisation that supports the children and families of prisoners in New Zealand she founded in 1988, has been praised around the world.

In 1983, her husband was sentenced to a long-term prison sentence and she was left with four children to care for. Not knowing how to cope, she reached out to God for help and He gave her a calling to start Pillars.

In 2011 she was awarded the New Zealand Order of Merit for services to the community and, in the same year, was called to the Beehive to receive the "Every Child Counts Award."

In 2018, she was awarded the highest Rotarian Award, the Paul Harris Fellowship.

the invisible sentence

She has spoken at many international and national conferences and given a TEDX talk.

In 2019, Pillars took out the Mitre 10 Community of the Year Award at the New Zealander of the Year Awards under Verna's leadership.

Verna worked with the Department of Corrections on child-friendly policies and services in prisons with the first Pillars Family Pathway Centres being set up in Christchurch and Invercargill prisons. The aim is for parents and children to bond and to understand and interrupt intergenerational cycles of offending.

Verna is a founding member of INCCIP, the International Coalition for Children of Incarcerated Parents and co-organised the inaugural conference in Rotorua, New Zealand in March 2017.

On 19 May 2018, Pillars celebrated its 30th anniversary the same day as Prince Harry and Meghan Markle's wedding.

Pillars was thrilled when the Prime Minister of New Zealand, Jacinda Ardern, announced that New Zealand's gift to the couple would be a donation of $5,000 to Pillars. The Duke and Duchess of Sussex visited Pillars to 'unwrap their gift' by presenting awards of excellence to four of the children.

Verna left Pillars in July 2020 after serving 32 years with the organisation when her position was made redundant and the head office was moved from Christchurch to Auckland. Verna says she will never retire.

Time away from Pillars has enabled her to write the first book of her memoirs. This is the first of many books and the second book will be about the setting up and leading Pillars.

Paul and Verna are directors of the company, Everyone Has a Story Ltd. They provide memoir and autobiography services so you can inspire the world with your story.

www.ingramcontent.com/pod-product-compliance
Lightning Source LLC
Chambersburg PA
CBHW021409290426
44108CB00010B/452